*From*

# Key Words of the Christian Life

## by Warren W. Wiersbe
General Director
Back to the Bible Broadcast

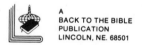

A
BACK TO THE BIBLE
PUBLICATION
LINCOLN, NE. 68501

**VICTOR**

**BOOKS** a division of SP Publications, Inc.
WHEATON, ILLINOIS 60187

Offices also in
Whitby, Ontario, Canada
Amersham-on-the-Hill, Bucks, England

70,000 printed to date—1982
(5-0853—70M—62)
ISBN 0-8474-6505-5

Printed in the United States of America

# Contents

Chapter 1

# The Power of Bible Words

In 1924 Adolf Hitler started writing his book *Mein Kampf*, which means "My Struggle." Some people ignored the book, and some laughed at it, but for every word in *Mein Kampf*, 125 people died in World War II. Never underestimate the power of words. A judge speaks, and a man is condemned or set free. A physician speaks, and a person has surgery or he goes home from the hospital. A government official speaks, and millions of dollars can be spent or withheld.

In our own personal lives we know the power of words—words that can bless us and words that can cut us and hurt us. Never underestimate the power of words. It is very important for us as Christians to know the meaning of Bible words. We need to understand these words and how they apply to our lives. Words such as justification, sanctification, propitiation, imputation and mediation—these words make up the technical vocabulary of the Christian life and are very important.

Our younger son is an electronics engineer. He designs those little chips that run the computers.

And he had to learn a very special vocabulary to do his job. My two older brothers were involved in mechanics, and they could run machines and fix things. They also had to learn a special vocabulary in order to do their job. I'm a pastor, a Bible teacher. I had to learn a special vocabulary to be able to handle the Word of God.

Some Christians say, "Don't bother me with doctrine; just give me the beautiful devotional thoughts of the Bible." But if devotion is not based upon correct doctrine, it is shallow, and it is not going to accomplish anything. It is merely shallow sentiment. In this first chapter I would like to explain why it is important for us to understand these key words of the Christian life.

The reason is very simple: When you understand these words, you are able to live what they teach. When we understand these key words of the Christian life, then we know what a Christian is, what God has done for us, and what God *wants* to do for us.

## God's Word Is Light

Perhaps the best way to approach this would be to introduce some of the pictures of the Word of God found in the Word of God. When we understand what God compares His Word to, then we'll know how important it is for us to know the meaning of Bible words and how they apply to our lives.

Let's begin with a very familiar picture of the Word of God—God's Word is light. "Thy word is a lamp unto my feet, and a light unto my path" (Ps. 119:105). What does a light do? A light enables us to see. When we understand these key words in the Bible, they are like lamps that guide us throughout all Scripture and throughout the Christian life.

God has revealed truth to us *in words*. "Now we have received, not the spirit of the world, but the spirit which is of God; that we might know the things that are freely given to us of God. Which things also we speak, not in the words which man's wisdom teacheth, but which the Holy Ghost [Spirit] teacheth; comparing spiritual things with spiritual" (I Cor. 2:12,13). In other words, God has revealed these things to us in words.

Revelation is simply God's work in communicating truth to us, truth that we could not discover any other way. Sometimes God revealed His truth in dreams or in visions; sometimes people heard a voice; sometimes they saw God in action. We today have God's Word, and we have God's words in the Bible. God has revealed His truth to us "that we might know the things that are freely given to us of God."

These words in the Bible are *inspired* words. Revelation is God's work in communicating truth to man, truth that man could never discover by himself. Inspiration is the supernatural work of the Holy Spirit in the lives of the writers of the Bible, enabling them to produce a trustworthy, written revelation. "All scripture is given by inspiration of God, and is profitable for doctrine, for reproof, for correction, for instruction in righteousness: that the man of

7

God may be perfect, throughly furnished unto all good works" (II Tim. 3:16,17). Inspiration means that the Holy Spirit of God so worked upon the writers of the Scriptures that they wrote a trustworthy revelation from God.

Second Peter 1:20,21 adds something to this: "Knowing this first, that no prophecy of the scripture is of any private interpretation. For the prophecy came not in old time by the will of man: but holy men of God spake as they were moved by the Holy Ghost." The Holy Spirit of God has given to us a dependable, trustworthy revelation of God in the Holy Scriptures, and God has revealed Himself through words.

In chapter 2 of II Peter we have a warning about false prophets and false teachers, and verse 3 makes an interesting statement: "And through covetousness shall they with feigned words make merchandise of you." That word "feigned" means pretending, counterfeit. The Greek word gives us our English word "plastic." Peter warned us about "plastic words." What are plastic words? Words that you can twist around to mean anything. Those who are false prophets and false teachers like to use our Christian *vocabulary*, but they do not use our Christian *dictionary*. They will talk about salvation, being born again, being justified and use the words that we use, but they don't use the same *meaning*. They twist words around to mean what they want them to mean in order to make merchandise out of you. You must be very, very careful of these religious counterfeits who are out to get something out of you instead of put something into you from the Lord. And they do it with plastic words.

God's Word is light; it enables us to see. If you want to know what's really going on in your life, in your world, then you'd better study the words in your Bible.

## God's Word Is Food

Second, God's Word is not only light, but God's Word is food. "Man shall not live by bread alone, but by every word that proceedeth out of the mouth of God" (Matt. 4:4). Food enables us to grow. As you grow in your knowledge of the Word of God, you can grow in your Christian life. "But grow in grace, and in the knowledge of our Lord and Saviour Jesus Christ" (II Pet. 3:18).

It is possible to grow in knowledge and not grow in grace. I have met people who have a great deal of Bible knowledge, but nobody can get along with them. They run from church to church, creating problems and trying to be important. It is possible to grow in knowledge but not grow in grace. However, when we are growing in knowledge, taught by the Holy Spirit, then we have to grow in grace. The same Holy Spirit who wrote the Word of God *writes* the Word of God in our hearts and enables us to reveal the fruit of the Spirit.

It is so important for us to grow by feeding on the Word of God. When you understand Bible doctrine—what it means to be justified, what it means to be sanctified, what propitiation means—and appropriate it into your own life, then you grow and mature in your Christian life. We read in Jeremiah

9

15:16: "Thy words were found, and I did eat them." Job said, "I have esteemed the words of his mouth more than my necessary food" (Job 23:12). In Hebrews 5:11-14 we are told that God's Word is milk and meat. And so we need God's Word as a light to guide us and as food to nourish us.

### God's Word Is a Tool

Third, God's Word is a tool for building. "Is not my word like as a fire? saith the Lord; and like a hammer that breaketh the rock in pieces?" (Jer. 23:29). Sometimes God's Word has to break down before it can build up. Sometimes God's Word has to burn before it can warm. But God's Word is like a hammer—it is a tool for breaking down the old life and building up the new life. It enables us to build the Church. Paul said, "Now, brethren, I commend you to God, and to the word of his grace, which is able to build you up, and to give you an inheritance among all them which are sanctified" (Acts 20:32). If you want to build your life, you must use tools, and the greatest tool of all is the Word of God. The better you understand the meaning of key Bible words, the more tools you will have in your "spiritual workshop" for getting the job done in building your own Christian life and helping to build the Church.

Church history proves that when the Word of God was given its free course, when there was faithful preaching and teaching of the Word of God, the Church grew with a strong missionary and evangelistic outreach.

The Word of God is light, it enables us to see. The Word of God is food, it enables us to grow. The Word of God is a tool, it enables us to build.

## God's Word Is a Weapon

The Word of God is also a weapon, it enables us to fight. Hebrews 4:12 tells us that the Word of God is "quick [living], and powerful, and sharper than any twoedged sword." Ephesians 6:17 reminds us that the Word of God is the sword of the Spirit: "And take . . . the sword of the Spirit, which is the word of God." You have discovered that the Christian life is not a playground, it is a battleground. There are false prophets and false teachers around us. There are false religions that are trying to make merchandise of you. Satan is out to get you. The world is out to get you. Satan is a liar, but God is the One who gives us truth.

It is important that you and I understand the words in the Word of God as weapons to fight battles. When Satan comes with one of his lies and tries to tell you that you have lost your salvation, you will be able to refute him. When you are going through a period of despondency and discouragement, you will be able to reach into your armory of weapons and fight the Devil.

If a doctor or a lawyer or an engineer has to learn a technical vocabulary to do his job, how much more important it is for us who have eternity in view! How much more important it is for us who are trying to win lost souls to know these Bible words and use them the way God wants us to use them.

11

My prayer is that this series of studies of Bible words will give all of us more light. I trust we will grow as we receive the spiritual food and that we will lay hold of the tools and the weapons for building and battling. It is my heart's desire that you and I shall grow in our spiritual intelligence as we understand the meaning of Bible words.

Chapter 2

# The Meaning and Method of Justification

Let's go back some four thousand years. We see a man sitting on an ash heap. His name is Job. He has a controversy with God because he doesn't quite understand what is going on, why he should be going through so much difficulty.

Did you know that in the King James Version of our Bible, there are more than 300 questions in the Book of Job? But the most important of all those questions is found in Job 9:2: "How shall a man be just with God?"

Now let's move up to the fall of the year 1515. An Augustinian monk is lecturing on the Book of Romans, and one verse comes to him with great power: "The just shall live by faith" (1:17). This was the beginning of change in Martin Luther's life and the beginning of the Reformation.

Now move up to May 24, 1738. An Anglican missionary (who wasn't sure of his own salvation) wrote these words in his journal: "In the evening I went very unwillingly to a society in Aldersgate Street where one was reading Luther's Preface to the Epistle to the Romans. About a quarter before nine while he was describing the change which God works in the heart through faith in Christ, I felt my heart strangely warmed. I felt I did trust in Christ, Christ alone for salvation, and assurance was given me that He had taken away my sins, even mine, and saved me from the law of sin and death." And thus did John Wesley receive the assurance of salvation through faith in Christ.

How can a man be just before God? *Justification* is one of the key words in the Christian life. The key verse is Romans 5:1: "Therefore being justified by faith, we have peace with God through our Lord Jesus Christ." We want to consider justification from three different aspects: The meaning of justification, the method of justification and the marks of justification.

## The Meaning of Justification

Justification is the gracious act of God in declaring righteous the sinner who believes on Jesus Christ. You should memorize this definition because it is important.

### Justification Is an Act

Notice, please, that justification is an *act*, not a process. No one Christian is more justified than any other Christian. If you are saved and your sister is saved, your sister and you are justified in the same way, and you have the same righteousness. Justification is not a process, it is an act. Instantly the

14

believer is given a righteous standing before God. It is the gracious act of *God*, it is not something that men do. No amount of self-effort, no amount of good works could ever bring a person to justification. We do not justify ourselves, it is God who justifies us.

## Justification Is Unchanging

Something else is true: Justification is *unchanging*. Once God has declared that we are righteous through Jesus Christ, the sin question is settled once and for all.

Justification is not the same as regeneration. (We shall be talking about regeneration in a later chapter.) Regeneration means being born again. Regeneration gives to us new life; justification gives us a new standing. Even a new-born baby has a legal standing before the law. Justification gives us a right standing before God; we are accepted in Jesus Christ.

Nor is justification the same as forgiveness. If God forgives me, and I go out and sin again, then I need to be forgiven again. But justification settles things permanently, eternally.

Nor is justification the same as pardon. A pardoned criminal is still a criminal. There is a record of his crimes in a file. Justification removes the guilt, justification changes our standing. This sounds remarkable, but it's true. Justification means not only that God forgets our sins—past, present and future—but justification means that God forgets *we were ever sinners*. He never again treats us as

15

sinners. We are not pardoned criminals, we are not people who have only been forgiven. It is true that pardon is a part of the Christian life, and so is forgiveness; but justification deals with the sin problem once and for all, giving us a right standing before God.

## Illustration of Justification

My friend Dr. Roy Gustafson has the finest illustration of justification I have ever heard. It seems that there was a man in England who put his Rolls-Royce on a boat and went across to the Continent to go on a holiday. While he was driving around Europe, something happened to the motor of his car. He cabled the Rolls-Royce people back in England and asked, "I'm having trouble with my car; what do you suggest I do?" Well, the Rolls-Royce people flew a mechanic over! The mechanic repaired the car and flew back to England and left the man to continue his holiday. As you can imagine, the fellow was wondering, "How much is this going to cost me?" So when he got back to England, he wrote the people a letter and asked how much he owed them. He received a letter from the office that read: "Dear Sir: There is no record anywhere in our files that anything ever went wrong with a Rolls-Royce." Now that's justification.

The Devil accuses you, you accuse yourself, maybe your friends accuse you; but God checks the file and says, "There is no record anywhere in this file that My child ever did anything wrong." That is justification—the gracious act of God in

16

declaring righteous one who believes in Jesus Christ.

## The Method of Justification

What is the method of justification? How can a holy God justify sinners? How can a holy God, as it were, overlook sin? Well, God does *not* overlook sin; God deals with it. There are four phrases you want to mark in your Bible in the Book of Romans, and these four phrases explain to us the method of justification.

### Freely by His Grace

Romans 3:24 says, "Being justified freely by his grace." How is God able to justify us? He justifies us *by grace, not by merit.* The word "freely" is translated "without a cause" in John 15:25. We are "justified without a cause by his grace." There is nothing in us that makes God want to justify us. Justification is purely an act of God's grace. Grace means favor that is not deserved and cannot be earned.

God justifies *the ungodly.* Romans 4:5 says, "But to him that worketh not, but believeth on him that justifieth the ungodly, his faith is counted for righteousness." In the Old Testament, God warned all of the judges that they should justify the righteous and condemn the wicked. Consider Deuteronomy 25:1: "If there be a controversy between men, and they come unto judgment, that the judges may judge them; then they shall justify the righteous, and condemn the wicked." If God did that to you and me, we would all be condemned forever. Why is it that God justifies the ungodly? For the simple rea-

17

son that *there are no godly*. "All have sinned, and come short of the glory of God" (Rom. 3:23).

## By Faith

Romans 3:28 says, "Therefore we conclude that a man is justified by faith without [apart from] the deeds of the law." Not only are we justified by grace, but we are justified *by faith*. Whenever you have *grace*, you have to have *faith*. Whenever you have Law, you have to have works. A person cannot be justified by keeping the Law. Romans 3:20 states, "Therefore by the deeds of the law there shall no flesh be justified in his sight: for by the law is the knowledge of sin [not the forgiveness of sin]."

We are justified by faith—faith in Christ, faith that comes from the heart. Faith is only as good as the object. Whatever you believe in may be wrong, no matter how sincere you are. Faith in a lie is false security; faith in the truth is true saving faith. We are justified by faith, not by works; and we are justified by grace, not by human merit.

## By His Blood

Romans 5:9 says, "Much more then, being now justified by his blood." Not only are we justified by grace and by faith, but we are justified by His blood. Somebody has to pay the price for sin. Justification is not some sort of fictional thing where God says, "I'll close my eyes and forget that they have sinned." God in His holiness must deal with sin. In order for God to justify the ungodly, He has to deal with their ungodliness. In order for us to be justified by faith, there has to be a Saviour for us to believe in. We are justified by His blood.

Romans 4:25, talking about our Lord Jesus, says, "Who was delivered for our offences, and was raised again for [on account of] our justification." Jesus died on the cross for our sins. He bore the penalty. Now God can be just and the justifier of those who believe in Christ.

The Devil comes and says, "How in the world can you declare Warren Wiersbe righteous?" And the answer comes, "By the blood of Jesus Christ." But what about Warren Wiersbe's sins? Jesus Christ died for those sins, and they have been taken care of. We are justified *by grace*, not by human merit; we are justified *by faith*, not by works of the Law; we are justified *by His blood* because Christ died for us.

Unto Life

Finally, Romans 5:18 says, "Therefore as by the offence of one [Adam] judgment came upon all men to condemnation; even so by the righteousness of one [Jesus Christ] the free gift came upon all men unto justification of life." That's a marvelous phrase—a justification which results in life. We are justified *unto life*.

Justification is not just something God does on His books. Justification results in a new standing and a new life. That new life is the result of regeneration. But justification makes possible our union with Christ, and this union is described in Romans 5:1-5. It is a life of peace and glory and joy.

Have you put your faith in Jesus Christ? What

are you trusting? You say, "I am trusting my church." That will not save you. "I am trusting my good works." That will not save you. We are justified by grace, not by human merit. We are justified by faith, not by works of the Law, including religious works. We are justified by His blood; He paid the price. This is a justification of life; we enter into a whole new life. And in our next chapter we shall examine the marks of justification and see what happens to the life of the person who trusts Jesus.

## Chapter 3

# The Marks of Justification

We are studying together the key words of the Christian life, the "doctrinal words" in the Bible that spell out for us what Christ has done for us and what He wants to do for us today. We began with a study of justification. Justification is the gracious act of God whereby He declares the believing sinner righteous in Christ. We have discussed the *meaning* of justification. It is an act, not a process; it is the act of God, not something that man does. And God's act justifies a person once and for all.

We also studied the *method* of justification. Justification is by grace, not by human merit. It is by faith and not by works—even religious works. It is by the blood of Jesus Christ, for He had to die so that our sins might be forgiven. And justification is unto life. It is not separated from life, it changes our lives.

Now we want to look at the *marks* of justification, and our key passage is Romans 5:1-5: "Therefore being justified by faith, we have peace with God through our Lord Jesus Christ: By whom also we have access by faith into this grace wherein we stand, and rejoice in hope of the glory of God. And not only so, but we glory in tribulations also: knowing that tribulation worketh patience; and patience, experience; and experience, hope: And hope maketh not ashamed; because the love of God is shed abroad in our hearts by the Holy Ghost which is given unto us."

The marks of justification in the believer's life are revealed in *relationships*. If you are truly justified by faith, then you are going to have a right relationship with *God*, a right relationship to *circumstances* and a right relationship to *other people*.

### Relationship With God

Let's begin with this right relationship with God described in Romans 5:1,2. You will recall that justification has to do with our standing before God. Justification does not *make* a person righteous; he is *declared* righteous. Now the consequence of this, of course, is a righteous life. The person who claims he is justified by faith but who lives a godless life is declaring that his lips are lying. Justification before God results in a changed life that is visible to other people.

#### Peace With God

Notice first of all that we have *peace with God*. "Therefore being justified by faith, we have peace with God" (Rom. 5:1). When we were unsaved, we were at war with God. "For if, when we were enemies, we were reconciled to God by the death of his Son, much more, being reconciled, we shall be saved by his life" (v. 10). There was a time when you and I were at enmity with God. In fact, Romans 8:7 informs us that the carnal mind, the fleshly mind, is enmity with God. The person who has never been born again doesn't think God's thoughts and doesn't desire what God desires; therefore, he is at war with God.

We cannot have peace until we first have righteousness. Justification has to do with righteousness. Because Jesus Christ died on the cross and rose again, we can have His righteousness when we put our faith in Him. In Psalm 85:10 we have this statement: "Mercy and truth are met together; righteousness and peace have kissed each other." Righteousness and peace "kiss each other" through Jesus Christ. As sinners, we have no righteousness of our own.

Our righteousness before God is as filthy rags (see Isa. 64:6). But when we receive His mercy—when we believe His truth—then righteousness is placed on our account. We are justified; therefore, we have peace. There can be no peace without righteousness.

The Prophet Isaiah makes this very clear in Isaiah 32:17: "And the work of righteousness shall be peace; and the effect of righteousness quietness and assurance for ever." So the first mark of justification, as far as my relationship to God is concerned, is that I have peace with God. I am not afraid of Him, although I have a reverence for Him. I am not at war with Him. I have a peace in my heart

23

that comes from a clear conscience, a clean heart, a righteous standing before God.

## Access to God

Second, not only is there peace with God, but there is *access to God*. We have peace with God through our Lord Jesus Christ, "by whom also we have access by faith" (Rom. 5:2). The unsaved person has no access to God because he has no standing before God. Those who have been justified by faith have access to God through the Lord Jesus Christ. We can come to the throne of grace, we can talk to our Heavenly Father, and we can fellowship with Him.

This access is into grace. "By whom also we have access by faith into this grace wherein we stand." Our standing before God is one of grace and not one of Law. Grace means that God provides for us; Law means I try to live to please God. Grace means God's resources available to Christians everywhere. Or grace means God's riches at Christ's expense. When you come by faith in Christ, you have access to the grace of God.

It is a marvelous thing to know that you are living by grace and not by Law. You are not living by your own merit or by your own ability, you are living by the grace of God that is sufficient for everything.

## Hope in the Glory of God

Something else is true. We not only have peace with God and access to God, but we rejoice in hope of the glory of God. The unsaved person has no hope. He has no future about which he can rejoice. When you trust Christ as your Saviour, you are standing in grace and you are rejoicing in hope. You have a bright future ahead of you because you are justified by faith.

What is this hope? The glory of God! Romans 3:23 informs us that all have sinned and come short of the glory of God. None of us measures up to God's glory. But when you become a Christian and you are justified by faith, then you can rejoice in the hope of the glory of God. You may be in difficult circumstances and you may hurt. Your body may be in pain. But you can still rejoice because, as a Christian, you have peace with God, you have access to God, you are standing in grace, you have hope. You can rejoice in that hope because one day you are going to share in the glory of God!

### Relationship to Circumstances

A second mark of justification is our relationship to circumstances (Rom. 5:3,4). The unsaved person is torn down by tribulations, but the believer is built up by tribulations. "And not only so, but we glory in tribulations also" (v. 3). That doesn't mean we go out and look for them, but when trials do come, we don't give up because we know that "tribulation worketh patience." The word "patience" doesn't mean sitting there very stoically, just passively enduring it. It means brave endurance that keeps you going. It is not someone sitting in a rocking chair; it is the soldier out on the battlefield who keeps on going when the going gets tough. When

25

you have been justified, when you are right with God, you are not bowled over by circumstances.

What life does to you depends upon what life finds in you. If you have peace with God within, if you have the grace of God, if you are rejoicing in the hope of the glory of God, then tribulation is going to work *for* you and not *against* you. Tribulation works "brave endurance," and endurance works "experience." That word "experience" means *tested character*. Nothing builds character like tribulation when you know God.

Circumstances *by themselves* do not build character. I have seen circumstances tear people down. But when you know God, circumstances can build character. The word "tribulation" comes from a Latin word, *tribulum*. A *tribulum* was a huge piece of wood (like a railroad tie) that had nails driven into it, and the oxen used to draw this piece of wood over the grain to thresh the grain. This is what tribulation does for us. Tribulation is God's way of separating the wheat from the chaff, the grain from the waste. And tribulation works *for* us because it develops brave endurance in us. When you have brave endurance, you start building character, and character produces hope. The most hopeful Christians I have met have been those who have gone through the threshing of tribulation.

When you have been justified by faith, you have a right relationship with God, and you have a right relationship to the circumstances around you. Circumstances are not tearing you down, they are building you up.

## Relationship to Others

Third, you have a right relationship to *others*. "And hope maketh not ashamed; because the love of God is shed abroad in our hearts by the Holy Ghost which is given unto us" (Rom. 5:5). This is a part of that "justification unto life" that is mentioned in verse 18. When you are justified by faith, when you trust the Saviour, the Holy Spirit comes into your life and you *know* that you are one of God's children. The Holy Spirit gives to you the fullness of God's love. "And hope does not disappoint, because the love of God [literally] has been poured out within our hearts through the Holy Spirit" (NASB). This means you allow love to rule in your relationships.

When you have this kind of love in your heart, it isn't hard to get along with other people, even difficult people. We have all experienced the change that took place because we trusted the Saviour. We replaced hatred, jealousy, envy and selfishness with love. The Holy Spirit began to produce in our lives the fruit of the Spirit listed here: *Love* in verse 5, *joy* in verse 2, *peace* in verse 1. The love of God, the peace of God and the joy that we have in God are all the result of justification by faith.

I would say it is a marvelous thing to be justified! There is no reason in all the world why we Christians should be walking around with long faces, with dismal expressions and always complaining. We have so much because we have trusted Christ as our Saviour! If you have been justified, you have a right relationship with God; you have peace with

God, not war; you have access to God; you have grace from God, and you can get through life with all of His power; you can rejoice in the hope of the glory of God.

More than that, you have a right relationship to circumstances. The difficult circumstances of life will not tear you down; they will build you up. They will build character and brave endurance, and they will give you a blessed hope. You will have a right relationship to others. The love of God shed abroad in your heart will pour out through your life, and you will find yourself getting along with people and glorifying God. These are the marks of justification.

Have you received Christ as your Saviour? Can you say, "Being justified by faith, *I* have peace with God"?

## Chapter 4

# Adoption into the Family of God

Since I was the last of four children in our home, I knew very little about seniority rights. Those of you who have had older brothers or sisters know what I am talking about. When I was born again into God's family, I was happy to discover that in His family there are no seniority rights. Instead, God has given to every one of His children a very wonderful experience known as adoption. An understanding of adoption is important if you and I are going to enjoy our Christian life to the full. To help us understand this doctrine, I'm going to try to answer three questions: What is adoption? What are the privileges of adoption? How can we make adoption work in our lives today?

### What Is Adoption?

*Question No. 1: What is adoption?* Adoption is the act of God by which He gives each of His children an adult standing in His family. Adoption is not the way you get into God's family. The only way to get into God's family is by *regeneration*, being born again. When a couple adopts a child, it is a beautiful experience. They can give that adopted child their name, their address, their home, their wealth; *but they cannot give that adopted child their nature.* That child will always have the nature of his parents. The only way to get into God's family is to have God's nature and share God's life, and that can come only by regeneration, being born again.

Adoption is not the way you get into God's family; adoption is the way you *enjoy* God's family. Adoption is the act of God by which He gives to each of His children an adult standing in His family. The instant you were saved, you received an adult standing, which means you have all the adult privileges. You also have adult responsibilities.

This means that you and I cannot use the length of time we have been saved as an excuse for being poor Christians. Someone may say, "Well, I have only been saved for four or five years; you can't expect too much of me." God says, "No, I expect of you what I expect of every one of My children. I am going to give you adult privileges, and I expect from you adult conduct and the fulfilling of adult responsibilities." That is what adoption is. Adoption means that the instant you were born into His family God gave you an adult standing.

### What Are the Privileges of Adoption?

*Question No. 2: What are the privileges of adoption?* Many of them are listed in Romans 8:14-17: "For as many as are led by the Spirit of God, they are the sons of God. For ye have not received the spirit of bondage again to fear; but ye have received the Spirit of adoption, whereby we cry, Abba, Father. The Spirit itself beareth witness with our spirit, that we are the children of God: And if children, then heirs; heirs of God, and joint-heirs with Christ; if so be that we suffer with him, that we may be also glorified together."

## Walking

We have listed here at least six privileges of adoption. I wonder how many of these privileges you and I have been claiming? First, there is the privilege of *walking*. "For as many as are led by the Spirit of God" (Rom. 8:14). That verb "led" means "willingly led." You can't lead a little baby because a baby cannot walk. A baby has to be carried. But when you enter God's family, you are adopted, and instantly you are able to walk.

The unsaved person walks according to the course of this world; he walks according to the prince of the power of the air; he walks in disobedience (see Eph. 2:2). But you and I have the privilege of walking in obedience, because we are led by the Spirit of God. God has a plan for our lives; He has a path on which we should walk. Romans 6:4 tells us we walk in newness of life. Romans 8:4 tells us that we walk not after the flesh but after the Spirit. We have the freedom and the blessing and the privilege of walking.

## Freedom

That leads to our second privilege—we have the privilege of *freedom*. "For ye have not received the spirit of bondage again to fear; but ye have received

31

the Spirit of adoption" (Rom. 8:15). Under the Law there was bondage. The Jewish nation had to obey, and if they did not obey, they would be judged.

Consider Galatians 4:1-7: "Now I say, That the heir, as long as he is a child, differeth nothing from a servant, though he be lord of all; but is under tutors and governors until the time appointed of the father. Even so we, when we were children, were in bondage under the elements of the world: But when the fulness of the time was come, God sent forth his Son, made of a woman, made under the law, to redeem them that were under the law, that we might receive the adoption of sons. And because ye are sons, God hath sent forth the Spirit of his Son into your hearts, crying, Abba, Father. Wherefore thou art no more a servant, but a son; and if a son, then an heir of God through Christ." There is a contrast here between being a servant and being a son.

The word "son" refers to a mature son, not just a little baby. When you are a child, you are under all kinds of rules and regulations. "Don't do this, and don't do that. Don't touch this, and don't go there." Sad to say, many Christians live like this; they live a life of legalistic bondage. Paul informs us that the Holy Spirit who has come into our lives is the Spirit of adoption. We have not received "the spirit of bondage again to fear" (Rom. 8:15). I suppose these two words best describe little children—*fear* and *bondage*. They are always afraid of something, and they are in bondage—they must always obey others. They are under the control of parents and teachers. You and I, as God's adopted children, have freedom from the Law. This does not mean we are lawless; it does mean that our relationship to our Father is one of love and not of bondage. We have freedom; we are able to walk.

## Speaking

Third, we have the privilege of *speaking*. Romans 8:15 states that we receive the Spirit of adoption "whereby we cry, Abba, Father." According to Galatians 4, when the Holy Spirit comes into our hearts, He cries Abba, Father, and then *we* are able to cry Abba, Father. No baby is born speaking. That would be a remarkable thing if a child could instantly speak. But when you were born into God's family, even though you were only one second old in the Lord, you were adopted and you had the privilege of speaking—speaking *to* God in prayer, in praise, in worship and speaking *for* God in witness.

## Assurance

The fourth privilege is found in Romans 8:16, the privilege of *assurance*. We know we are God's children. Notice what it says: "The Spirit itself beareth witness with our spirit, that we are the children of God." No little baby knows it is a baby. It doesn't even know it is a human being. It has to grow into this knowledge. No baby knows who his parents are. A baby gets to know very early that certain people are very close to him and are very meaningful to him, but he doesn't know how to call them father or mother. When you and I were born again and adopted, instantly we knew we were God's children. Instantly we knew who our Father was and were able to look up and say, "Abba, Father." The word "Abba" is equivalent to our word "daddy." "Abba" expresses our close, intimate, loving relationship with our Heavenly Father.

So we have the privilege of walking, the privilege of freedom, the privilege of speaking and the privilege of assurance.

### Inheritance

We have a fifth privilege, the privilege of *inheritance*. Romans 8:17 says, "If children, then heirs; heirs of God, and joint-heirs with Christ." No baby can inherit anything. If the parents die, and they leave their estate to their baby, that baby has to be under trustees until he can legally inherit the wealth. You and I do not have to wait to mature to inherit our wealth. If that were the case, we would never grow up. *We need that spiritual wealth now in order to grow up.* In Romans 8:17 we are told that we are now the heirs of God and joint-heirs with Christ. That means everything we inherit comes through Christ. We have two names on the check: Our Lord Jesus signs the check, and we have to sign the check.

This is what prayer is all about. This is why we come "in the name of Jesus," because apart from Him we can inherit nothing. As a Christian, you are rich today. Ishmael was Abraham's firstborn son, born of Hagar, but Ishmael was born poor. Isaac was born rich. You and I were born rich in Jesus Christ. We have the riches of His grace, the riches of His wisdom and the riches of His mercy. We can draw upon all of His riches in glory by Christ Jesus.

## Suffering

Finally, we have the privilege of *suffering*. Romans 8:17 says, "If so be that we suffer with him, that we may be also glorified together." We do everything we can to shield babies from suffering. If a baby starts to suffer, everybody drops everything to make that baby comfortable. But God allows His children to suffer, because we aren't babies. He is treating us as adults.

We need suffering because it builds character. We need suffering because it builds spiritual muscles. Suffering teaches us much about the grace of God, and suffering prepares us for future glory. "If so be that we suffer with him, that we may be also glorified together." God gives us the privileges of suffering because He wants us to grow up. The ultimate privilege of life is to be entrusted with God's glory. God puts us through suffering that He might be able to share His glory with us. That is an amazing thing!

Are you living up to your privileges? If you are a Christian, you have been adopted, you have an adult standing in the family of God. With this standing comes responsibility. We don't run away from suffering. We don't waste our inheritance. We are sure that we are born again, and we share this with others. We have the privilege of speaking to and for God and the freedom of walking with God. What privileges we have!

## How Can We Enjoy Adoption?

*Question No. 3: How can we enjoy adoption now?*

### Believe

To begin with, *believe that it is true.* Adoption is not a feeling, it is a fact. Just believe that it is true. Look at yourself in the mirror and say, "You are being treated as an adult son, an adult daughter, not as a little baby." God does not pamper His children. He will have no pampered children at all, because pampered children cannot be used for His glory. So just believe it and say, "Thank God I have been adopted; I have an adult standing before God. All these privileges are mine."

### Yield

Second, *yield to the Holy Spirit,* for He is the Spirit of adoption. He is the One who will make all of this real to you. In Romans 8:2 He is called the Spirit of life. In Romans 8:13 we see He is the Spirit of death—He puts to death the deeds of the body. Yield to the Holy Spirit and claim God's promise by faith. The blessing is there; it is true, it is real. Start treating yourself the way God treats you. Look upon yourself as an adult son or daughter in His family. Stop pampering yourself. Stop whimpering. Stop asking God to give you toys; ask Him to give you tools and weapons, because there is a Church to build and a battle to fight. It is a marvelous thing to be adopted and to be rich in the Lord Jesus Christ.

Chapter 5

# Regeneration: The New Birth

The English word "regeneration" simply means new birth, renewal or restoration. It is used only twice in our Authorized Version of the Bible. In Titus 3:5 we read about a *personal* regeneration: "Not by works of righteousness which we have done, but according to his mercy he saved us, by the washing of regeneration, and renewing of the Holy Ghost." Do not allow that word "washing" to make you think of baptism, because regeneration— being born again—does not come through baptism. The word "washing" in Titus 3:5 is parallel to the word "renewing" at the end of the verse: "By the washing of regeneration, and renewing of the Holy Ghost." Personal regeneration is the work of the Holy Spirit in the life of the person who trusts Christ as his Saviour. So there is a personal regeneration.

But there is also a *universal* regeneration. Our Lord speaks about this in Matthew 19:28: "And Jesus said unto them, Verily I say unto you, That ye which have followed me, in the regeneration when the Son of man shall sit in the throne of his glory, ye also shall sit upon twelve thrones, judging the

37

twelve tribes of Israel." Our Lord tells us there is going to be a future regeneration of this world when He will sit upon a throne and He will judge and there will be glory and perfection.

The word "regeneration" (born again) simply means the act of God by which *new life* is imparted to the person who trusts Christ as his Saviour. Justification gives me a *righteous standing* before God; adoption gives me *an adult standing* before God, but regeneration gives me the *life* of God, the *nature* of God, in my very being.

Regeneration does not simply put us back to where we would have been had Adam never sinned. Regeneration is birth into a brand-new life; it is sharing the very life of God. It is not just a reformation. If regeneration were only reformation, then the next time you sinned, you would have lost it. No, regeneration is that act of God whereby the very life of God is communicated to those who trust Christ as their Saviour.

The classic text on regeneration is John 3. "There was a man of the Pharisees, named Nicodemus, a ruler of the Jews: the same came to Jesus by night, and said unto him, Rabbi, we know that thou art a teacher come from God: for no man can do these miracles that thou doest, except God be with him. Jesus answered and said unto him, Verily, verily, I say unto thee, Except a man be born again, he cannot see the kingdom of God. Nicodemus saith unto him, How can a man be born when he is old? can he enter the second time into his mother's womb, and be born? Jesus answered, Verily, verily, I say unto thee, Except a man be born of water and of the Spirit, he cannot enter into the kingdom of God. That which is born of the flesh is flesh; and that which is born of the Spirit is spirit. Marvel not that I said unto thee, Ye must be born again. The wind bloweth where it listeth [will], and thou hearest the sound thereof, but canst not tell whence it cometh, and whither it goeth: so is every one that is born of the Spirit. Nicodemus answered and said unto him, How can these things be?" (vv. 1-9).

This passage has been preached upon and taught for many, many centuries. It is familiar to us. In fact, I trust its familiarity does not rob us of its true meaning. There are several facts about regeneration, the new birth, that need to be understood, and they are given to us in this passage.

### Reality of the New Birth

First of all, we are confronted with *the reality of the new birth*. The word "born" is used eight times in John 3:1-9. Jesus was talking about a real experience—the reality of the new birth. There are those who tell us that this experience of regeneration is psychological, that people can even have this kind of experience apart from faith in Jesus Christ. There are false religions and psychological approaches to religion which tell us that the new birth happens because of some psychological experience. The new birth is a reality; it is as real an experience as physical birth.

No one would deny his own physical birth, and

39

we do not have to deny our spiritual birth. Jesus said that the new birth is a reality. If you would interview people who trusted Jesus, you would find out how real it is. Ask Peter; he knew what it was to trust in Jesus Christ and to experience this new birth. In his letters Peter tells us about this matter of being born again. Matthew, the publican, had his life radically changed because he trusted Christ and experienced the new birth. The thief on the cross turned to Jesus and said, "Remember me, Lord, when You come into Your kingdom" (see Luke 23:42). Because of his faith in Christ he was born again. Ask him whether or not it is a real experience.

Ask the Apostle Paul. Saul of Tarsus, the leading young Jewish rabbi of his day, was persecuting the church when he met Jesus Christ. He put his faith in Jesus Christ, and he was born again. It was a real experience.

When our Lord was ministering here on earth, everybody had some answers to the problems of life. The Romans said the way to solve life's problems is through *law*, and you back up that law with the military. The Greeks said, "No, the way to solve problems is with *wisdom*. People need schools, understanding and philosophy." Of course the Jewish people said, "No, the answer is *religion*. But you need sacrifices, a priesthood, the temple." Jesus said the answer is in the heart. Law will never change the heart; wisdom will never change the heart; religion will never change the heart, but regeneration will. The reality of the new birth, the good news of the Gospel, is this: *You can start all over again!* You do not have to stay the way you are; you can start over again. Because there is such a thing as regeneration, you can be born again.

## Simplicity of the New Birth

Next is *the simplicity of the new birth.* Our Lord Jesus used birth as a simple illustration of what happens when a person is saved. Even though he was a great teacher of Israel, Nicodemus unfortunately misunderstood what our Lord was talking about. "How can a man be born when he is old?" asked Nicodemus. "Can he enter the second time into his mother's womb and be born?" (see John 3:4). Our Lord was talking about something *spiritual,* but Nicodemus interpreted this as something *physical.*

In John 4, when our Lord was talking to the woman at the well, He talked about living water. He said, "If you ask Me, I will give you water, and you will never be thirsty again" (see vv. 10,14). He was speaking spiritually, but she took Him literally and materially, and she said, "How can You give me any water? You don't even have a vessel to draw with" (see v. 11).

In John 6, our Lord was talking about eating the Bread of Life, feeding on His flesh and His blood. The Jews were offended by this. But He wasn't speaking in material terms. He tells us Himself that it is the Spirit that gives life; the flesh profits nothing (v. 63).

When Jesus spoke about birth, Nicodemus took Him literally. Jesus replied in John 3:5,6, "Except a

41

man be born of water [physical birth] and of the Spirit, he cannot enter into the kingdom of God. That which is born of the flesh [physical birth] is flesh." Our Lord was saying, "Nicodemus, please don't major on the physical and the material—I'm talking in spiritual terms."

Two parents create this new birth—the Spirit of God and the Word of God, according to James 1:18 and I Peter 1:23. We are born again by the Word of God, the living Word of God. The Spirit of God takes the Word of God and reveals the Son of God. And when you trust Jesus Christ as your Saviour, a miracle takes place in your heart—regeneration; you are born again. The two "spiritual parents" who accomplish this birth are the Spirit of God and the Word of God.

The Bible makes it very clear in John 1:13 that we are not born of the flesh, we are not born of the will of man, we are not born of our own efforts. No baby is born of his own effort. No baby can conceive himself. We are born by the Spirit of God.

Mystery is involved. I will confess that. In John 3:8 Christ says, "The wind bloweth where it listeth [will], and thou hearest the sound thereof, but canst not tell whence it cometh, and whither it goeth: so is every one that is born of the Spirit." He is not comparing the wind to the Holy Spirit, although that is a valid illustration. *He is comparing the believer to the wind:* "So is every one that is born of the Spirit." There is mystery to physical birth; there is mystery to spiritual birth. But just think of how simple it is: Trust Jesus Christ, and you shall be born again.

42

## Dignity of the New Birth

A third fact comes to our attention—*the dignity of the new birth*. The word translated "born again" can be translated "born *from above*." We are born children of the King, children of God. "But as many as received him, to them gave he power to become the sons of God, even to them that believe on his name" (John 1:12). "Behold, what manner of love the Father hath bestowed upon us, that we should be called the sons [children] of God" (I John 3:1). The dignity of the new birth is an amazing thing.

Children like to be proud of their parents. If we have some relative who is somebody important, we like to talk about it. We become name-droppers. You and I share the dignity of the new birth; we are the children of God—the God who created the universe, the God and Father of our Lord Jesus Christ. We are in His family, we share His nature. I have the nature of my parents, and my children have my nature. We have God's nature within because we have been born from above, and this new nature creates a new disposition.

When you are one of God's children and you share God's nature, you live the way God wants you to live. God is love, and so we love; God is light, and so we walk as children of light. We share His nature and His life, and people can see a difference in our lives.

## Urgency of the New Birth

Finally, *the urgency of the new birth*. Jesus said, "Ye must be born again" (John 3:7). It is not a suggestion, it is a commandment. It is not an idea that we can toy with; it is absolutely urgent—we must be born again. The new birth is instantaneous, it is not a process. There may be a process of preparation; you may have a desire to know God or a concern about getting rid of sin. But the birth itself is instantaneous, supernatural and permanent.

Once you are born, you can't be unborn. You may be disobedient; you may not grow as you should, but you cannot be unborn. Our spiritual birth is a permanent, supernatural birth, and there is urgency to it. "Except a man be born again, he cannot see the kingdom of God" (v. 3). The god of this world blinds those who believe not. Until you are born again, you cannot see what you are missing; you cannot see what you really are; you cannot see all that God has for you. You must be born again not only to *see* the kingdom of God but to *enter* the kingdom of God. "Except a man be born of water [physical birth] and of the Spirit, he cannot enter into the kingdom of God" (v. 5).

When you were born the first time, you entered into the kingdom of sin and Satan. You lived according to the course of this world, and you followed the dictates of Satan. But when you entered the kingdom of God through regeneration, then you became a part of that kingdom which is wonderful, eternal and glorious. The only way to escape eternal judgment is through faith in Christ. "For God so loved the world, that he gave his only begotten Son, that whosoever believeth in him should not perish, but have everlasting life" (v. 16). That verse *begins* with

44

love, but it *ends* with perish—"should not perish, but have everlasting life."

Have you been thinking about this? Has God been talking to you? The *reality* of the new birth is that you can change; God will change you when you trust Christ. The *simplicity* of the new birth is that it is not through religion or good works but through trusting the Saviour. Imagine becoming a child of God and enjoying the *dignity* of the new birth! The *urgency* of the new birth is that you *must* be born again. If God has been talking to you about this, then open your heart now to Jesus Christ.

Chapter 6

# Propitiation: Satisfaction of God's Holiness

Propitiation is one of those technical words in the New Testament that we need to understand. "Whom God hath set forth to be a propitiation through faith in his blood, to declare his righteousness for the remission of sins that are past, through the forbearance of God" (Rom. 3:25).

When you walk into the Book of Romans, you walk into a court of law. There you and I stand before God, the Judge. We are guilty. We are *criminals* who are guilty of disobeying God's Law. Our standing before God has been forfeited. Not only are we criminals, we are *prisoners*—we are in bondage. Our condition, our state, is one of bondage and one of agony. I cannot conceive of a lost sinner's enjoying life, for he has nothing to enjoy. The very sword of God's judgment hangs over his head. We are *condemned,* we face the wrath of God.

When we look *back,* we realize we are guilty of disobedience. When we look *around,* we realize we are prisoners. When we look *ahead,* we realize we are condemned, we have no future. This the Book of Romans teaches very clearly.

How can we get out of this terrible plight? We are helpless, we can't do it ourselves. The Judge may love us and want to help us all that he can, but he has to obey the Law. The only solution is that someone qualified can come in, obey the Law, fulfill the righteous demands of the Law and set us free. Of course, that person is Jesus Christ. This is what propitiation is all about.

### Definition of Propitiation

Let us consider this wonderful doctrine from three different aspects. First of all, the *definition* of propitiation. Propitiation is the work of Jesus Christ on the cross by which He satisfied God's holiness so God could extend mercy to lost sinners. If you look up the word "propitiation" in an English dictionary, you will find it defined as "appeasing someone's anger." Some people have the idea that God the Father is angry at lost sinners. They think He is sitting in heaven waiting to throw thunderbolts upon people who have disobeyed Him. Then God the Son comes up and says, "Now, Father, please don't be angry! I will go and die for these sinners, and this will appease Your wrath." Nothing could be further from the truth.

To begin with, Jesus Christ and His Father and the Holy Spirit *work together in this whole great plan of salvation.* It is not that one wants to condemn and the other wants to forgive. When Jesus went to the cross of Calvary, the Father was there.

47

It is true the Father forsook His Son when His Son was made sin, but that was just for a brief moment when our Saviour cried out, "My God, my God, why hast thou forsaken me?" (Matt. 27:46). The Father and the Son and the Holy Spirit worked together in the plan of salvation. Propitiation does not mean that Jesus Christ came to appease God's anger.

Some people have the idea that, because of His death on the cross, our Lord turned God's wrath into love. Again, nothing could be further from the truth. Our God is a God of judgment. We want to be very clear about that. Throughout the Bible you find the revelation of the wrath of God as well as the mercy of God. There are almost 20 Hebrew words in the Old Testament translated wrath. There are more than 500 references to wrath and judgment just in the Old Testament. Our Father in heaven is a loving Father, but He is also a holy Father. He is love (I John 4:8), but He is also light (1:5). God's anger does not turn into love because this would mean that God is changing, and God does not change. Propitiation does not mean appeasing God's anger; propitiation does not mean turning God's wrath into love. His wrath is a holy wrath; His judgment is a holy judgment. Because He loves holiness and hates sin, He has to be a God of judgment.

Propitiation means that Christ satisfied the holiness of God so that He is able to extend grace and mercy to lost sinners. God is a holy God, and because He is holy sin has to be punished. God cannot break His own Law. If for one instant God broke His Law, the universe would fall apart. All of God's attributes are consistent. His wisdom does not fight against His power. His power does not fight against His grace. His grace does not fight against His holiness. There is a cooperation, a consistency, a unity about the character of God.

You and I are not consistent. At times we are overly sentimental and loving; at other times we are overly angry and unforgiving. God is not this way. God's attributes are consistent and unified, and so there is no need for Him to lay one aside for the other. God's holiness demands that sin be punished. God cannot lie, God cannot break His own Law. His love moves Him to save the sinner, but His love is a *holy* love, and this is where propitiation comes in.

Jesus Christ satisfied the demands of the Law. Propitiation describes the *God-ward* work of Christ on the cross—He paid the penalty for the broken Law. The Law was satisfied. He bore the judgment of the guilty sinner, and sinners now can be justified. Forgiveness is now available because of God's grace. There is no condemnation because Jesus Christ has died.

The old Puritan theologian, John Owen, has summarized propitiation in four simple statements. First, there is *an offense to be removed.* Sinners have offended a holy God. Second, there is *an offended person* to be dealt with—God the Father. God the Father simply cannot close His eyes like some doting grandfather and say, "Well, I'll forget

49

all about it." A holy God has to deal with sin. Third, *the person who has offended has to be pardoned.* If he is not pardoned, he is condemned. In order for this to happen, *a sacrifice has to be offered.* So there is an offense to be removed, an offended person to be satisfied, an offending person to be pardoned, and a sacrifice to be made to make this all possible. This is the meaning of propitiation.

## Demonstration of Propitiation

A *demonstration* of propitiation is found in Leviticus 16. You are acquainted, I'm sure, with the great Day of Atonement in Leviticus 16. Once a year the high priest laid aside his beautiful garments, and he offered sacrifices for his own sins. Then he set apart two goats: One goat was chosen to die, and the other goat was chosen to stay alive. The high priest would kill the goat that was set aside for sacrifice and take the blood of that goat into the Holy of Holies. This was the only time in the year when the high priest was allowed to go into the Holy of Holies. He sprinkled the blood on the mercy seat. The mercy seat was that beautiful, golden covering on the ark of the covenant. At each end of the mercy seat there was a golden cherub, positioned as though looking down into the ark. In the ark were the tables of the Law. When the priest came in and sprinkled the blood upon that mercy seat, the blood covered the broken Law.

Then he would go out and put his hands on the head of the living goat and confess the sins of the people of Israel. That living goat was then taken out into the wilderness, turned loose and never seen again. Together these two goats made up a sin offering. It is a picture to us of John 1:29: "Behold the Lamb of God, which taketh away the sin of the world."

The Lord Jesus Christ died on the cross; His blood turned the throne of judgment into a throne of grace, a mercy seat. In fact, the word "propitiation" is translated mercy seat in Hebrews 9:5. God's justice has been satisfied, and now God can forgive our sins and take them from us as far as the east is from the west. The Law has been satisfied, and God is "free" to extend pardon and mercy. He can be just as He forgives our sins.

## Dynamic of Propitiation

I want to close this chapter by talking about the *dynamic* of propitiation. If you know Jesus as your Saviour, then you have all of the blessings that are wrapped up in propitiation. What are they?

### Sinners Can Be Saved

First of all, *sinners can be saved from judgment.* We read in I John 4:10: "Herein is love, not that we loved God, but that he loved us, and sent his Son to be the propitiation for our sins." In I John 2:2 we read these words: "And he is the propitiation for our sins; and not for our's only, but also for the sins of the whole world." Propitiation says that sinners can be saved from judgment, and not just a few sinners—propitiation is available to the whole world.

When the Lord Jesus Christ rose from the dead

51

and the tomb was left empty, Mary came to the tomb and stood outside weeping. When she stooped and looked in the tomb, she saw two angels—one at the head and one at the feet of where the body had been lying, *just like the mercy seat* (see John 20:11,12). The garments our Lord had been wrapped in were lying there empty, because He had arisen from the dead. But at each end of that stone slab there was an angel. It looked just like the mercy seat! Because Jesus died for us, sinners can be saved from judgment.

You are ready to give up. You are ready to quit. Sin has gotten such a hold on your life that you don't know what to do. I have good news for you; Christ is the propitiation for our sins, and not for ours only but for the sins of the whole world. This is a good motivation to get the Gospel out to the whole world. Your church's ministry and your ministry ought to be one of worldwide missions as well as witnessing to people here at home. So the dynamic of propitiation is that sinners can be saved from judgment by trusting Jesus Christ.

## Believers Can Be Forgiven

Second, *believers can be forgiven when they sin.* First John 2:1,2 says, "My little children, these things write I unto you, that ye sin not. And if any man sin, we have an advocate with the Father, Jesus Christ the righteous: and he is the propitiation for our sins." Because Jesus Christ died for our sins, He met the holy demands of God's just Law, and we can be forgiven. We don't have to be saved all over again; we are forgiven. We can come to the Lord Jesus Christ and confess our sins. He forgives us and restores us because we come to the mercy seat where His blood has been applied.

## We Can Find Strength

There is a third dynamic to propitiation. It not only means forgiveness for lost sinners, a message for the whole world and the assurance of forgiveness when we sin, but it means that *we can find strength for living at the mercy seat.* Hebrews 4:16 says, "Let us therefore come boldly unto the throne of grace, that we may obtain mercy, and find grace to help in time of need." The mercy seat is the place where we meet God, where we meet Jesus Christ and where we can find grace for the demands of life.

So the Lord Jesus Christ is our propitiation. He has provided all that is necessary for salvation, for daily forgiveness, for motivation to witness to the whole world and for strength for daily living. When you have used your hymnal in church, I'm sure you have seen the name William Cowper. He was a discouraged man, a very nervous fellow, ready to give up. And he said in one of his writings, on a day when he was extremely distraught, "I flung myself into a chair near the window, and seeing a Bible there, ventured once more to apply to it for comfort and instruction. The first verse I saw was the 25th of the 3rd of Romans: 'Whom God hath set forth to be a propitiation through faith in his blood.' I saw the sufficiency of the atonement He had made, my pardon sealed in His blood, and all the fulness and

53

completeness of His justification. In an instant I believed and received the peace of the gospel."

He wrote these words:

> There is a fountain filled with blood
> Drawn from Immanuel's veins,
> And sinners plunged beneath that flood
> Lose all their guilty stains.

"Whom God hath set forth to be a propitiation through faith in his blood" (Rom. 3:25).

## Chapter 7

# Imputation: God Credits Our Account

So important is eternal life that the Bible gives us many illustrations so that no one will miss the message. To the farmers, Jesus talked about soil and seed. To the shepherds, He talked about sheep. To beggars, He talked about a great feast that God had spread. To lawyers, He talked about justification. To the housewife, He talked about a coin that had been lost and had to be found. But when you use the word "imputation," you find God speaking to the banker, because this is a financial term.

Romans 4:1-8 says, "What shall we say then that Abraham our father, as pertaining to the flesh, hath found? For if Abraham were justified by works, he hath whereof to glory; but not before God. For what saith the scripture? Abraham believed God, and it was counted unto him for righteousness. Now to him that worketh is the reward not reckoned of grace, but of debt. But to him that worketh not, but believeth on him that justifieth the ungodly, his faith is counted for righteousness. Even as David also describeth the blessedness of the man, unto whom

55

God imputeth righteousness without [apart from] works, saying, Blessed are they whose iniquities are forgiven, and whose sins are covered. Blessed is the man to whom the Lord will not impute sin."

Our English word "imputation" comes from the Latin word which means "to reckon, or credit, to one's account." When you go to the bank or the savings and loan association and deposit money, imputation takes place. They deposit that on your account, and they write it on your record.

We want to study imputation from three different aspects—first by way of *explanation,* then by way of *example* and finally by way of *experience.*

## Explanation of Imputation

The easiest way to understand imputation is simply to see two record books, two bankbooks. One of them has Christ's name on it, and the other has Adam's name on it. The record book for our Lord Jesus Christ is perfect—there is no indebtedness whatsoever. He is absolutely righteous, and His record is spotless. But alas, the record book for Adam is imperfect—he is bankrupt! He has sinned and come short of the glory of God.

*Our* record is Adam's record because we are the children of Adam. Genesis 5:1 says, "This is the book of the generations of Adam." The entire Old Testament is "the book of the generations of Adam," and everyone named in the book is a failure. Then you turn to Matthew 1:1 and read: "The book of the generation of Jesus Christ." God opens a new book, and that book is perfect, because His Son's name is on it.

What can you and I do about this imperfect record that is on our account? As far as God's spiritual bank is concerned, we are bankrupt—we fall short. God has audited the books and discovered that you and I do not have anything with which to pay for our indebtedness. What shall we do about it?

Well, we could *ignore* it, and most people do. Most people don't think about their debt to God. They have broken His Law; they have gone beyond His barriers. He has said, "This far and no farther," and they have said, "We're going to do it anyway." Then they try to ignore their disobedience. But a day of reckoning is coming, and that day may be soon.

A man can work for a bank and secretly be stealing money and falsifying the records, but eventually a day of reckoning comes, and he is caught. So we can ignore it, but the day of reckoning is going to come.

We could try to *change it ourselves*, but we are too bankrupt to do this. We simply do not have the spiritual capital necessary to wipe out the spiritual debt that we have to God. Can we *destroy the book?* No, that book is in God's hands; no one can destroy that record. How, then, can we solve the problem of our spiritual bankruptcy—the debt that we have to God? Well, the answer is *imputation,* and Jesus Christ is the One who comes with the solution. What did He do?

## Christ Took Our Debt

First of all, *He took our debt.* That is a remarkable thing. When our Lord Jesus Christ came to earth, He came to die. God made Christ to be sin for us—He who knew no sin. Why? "That we might be made the righteousness of God in him" (II Cor. 5:21). In Isaiah 53:12 we are told that He was reckoned among the transgressors. This is quoted in Mark 15:28. That word "reckon" means *counted.* In other words, He was counted as a transgressor. He was made poor that we might become rich (II Cor. 8:9). So He took our debt.

## He Gave Us His Righteousness

But that leaves me with a problem. If He takes my debt, then the next time I sin, I go back into debt again. So He did something else. He not only took our debt, but *He credited to our account His own righteousness.* Romans 4:6 says, "Even as David also describeth the blessedness of the man, unto whom God imputeth righteousness without [apart from] works." Imputation means *putting it to our account.*

You must not confuse imputation with impartation. Let me explain. Justification means God puts His righteousness on our account. This is righteousness *imputed.* Right in the middle of that word "impute" you have p-u-t, *put*—righteousness put to our account. But sanctification is righteousness *imparted*—God shares His righteousness in our lives and enables us to live a holy life. So Jesus Christ paid our debt; He assumed our bankruptcy.

Second, He credited His righteousness to our account so that we have the righteousness of Christ on our record. That is a remarkable thing.

But once again, I ask the question, What about the next time I sin? Romans 4:8 takes care of that: "Blessed is the man to whom the Lord will not impute sin." Once the righteousness of Christ has been put on our record, *how could God ever record sin?* Can He record our sin along with the righteousness of Christ? Of course not. The righteousness of Jesus Christ is written on our record. "Blessed are they whose iniquities are forgiven, and whose sins are covered. Blessed is the man to whom the Lord will not impute sin" (vv. 7,8). So there is the negative and the positive. Negatively, He took our debt; positively, He credits His righteousness to our account. He does not record our sin.

### Example of Imputation

Now let's look at imputation by way of example. The most beautiful example of imputation is found in a little letter that Paul wrote to his friend Philemon. I think you probably know the story. Philemon had a slave named Onesimus. Onesimus stole something from his master, Philemon, and fled to the city of Rome, trying to hide. In the providence of God, Onesimus met Paul and was converted. Paul wrote this letter to Philemon on behalf of Onesimus, because he wanted Philemon to forgive Onesimus and to restore him.

Onesimus is a picture of the lost sinner. He was a

59

slave—he had no freedom of his own, he was in bondage. He was a thief; he had robbed his master. A slave was not treated with much kindness and mercy in those days. He deserved to die. He tried to run away. He was a lawbreaker, and he was caught. And yet Paul loved this man, and God loved this man, so Paul wrote to Philemon these words, in verse 18: "If he hath wronged thee, or oweth thee ought, put that on mine account." Isn't that thrilling? Paul was saying, "I want you to impute his debt to me. He stole from you, and he has probably sold what he had stolen and spent the money. He is broke, he is bankrupt, but you put that on my account." That is imputation.

But that is not enough. Verse 17 says, "If thou count me therefore a partner, receive him as myself." That is the positive part. He said, "When Onesimus comes home, don't see Onesimus, see Paul. Receive him the way you would receive me. Receive him as myself."

The Lord Jesus Christ did that for us. He said to God the Father, "Warren Wiersbe is bankrupt. He couldn't begin to pay his debt. Put it on My account." He died for me. And now He says to God the Father, "Whenever you see Warren Wiersbe, see Your own Son. Receive him as You would receive Me." That is imputation. It is marvelous, isn't it, that God should not only pay our debt but that He should give us His righteousness? Then He says, "Your sins and your iniquities will I remember no more. I am no longer keeping a record."

God does keep a record of our *works*, and of course our sins affect our works. We must not think that because God is not keeping a record of our sins we can freely go out and sin. Of course, no born-again Christian wants to deliberately, habitually sin. In fact, the person who lives like that would be giving evidence he has never really been born again. But this doctrine of imputation encourages us to seek cleansing when we do sin.

## Experience of Imputation

Now let's look at imputation by way of experience. How can we make this work in our lives?

### Admit Your Debt

First of all, *admit your debt.* If you have never been born again, if you have never been saved, just admit that you are in debt, that you are bankrupt and that you can't pay it yourself.

You will remember in Luke 7:36-50, Jesus had a meeting with a Pharisee. While He was having dinner with the Pharisee, a woman of the streets came in and wept and washed our Lord's feet. The Pharisee was offended. But Jesus told a story about two people who were in debt. In modern language, one owed a thousand dollars and one owed ten dollars. But the man to whom they owed this debt freely forgave them both. Now Jesus said to this Pharisee, "Which one of those two people is going to love him the most?" He said, "Well, I suppose the one who had the most forgiven." But Simon didn't realize that *he* himself was in debt. He said, "Oh, this woman of the streets, she is in debt to God. She has broken God's Law. But Simon the Pharisee hasn't." Jesus said, "Now, wait a minute. You are just as much in debt as she is and maybe more, because you don't see it the way she does. Furthermore, you are just as bankrupt." Admit your debt, and receive by grace God's gift of righteousness.

## Don't Record Your Own Sins

Second, *don't keep books on yourself.* Some Christians are always remembering what God has forgotten, and they are forgetting what God wants them to remember. It is good for us to say, "Search me, O God, and know my heart" (Ps. 139:23). But it is also good for us not to keep a record of our sins. God is not keeping a record of our sins, so why should we? The Devil loves to have us do this. Satan enjoys it when God's people wallow around in self-pity, remembering their past sins, and get discouraged and feel guilty. God has forgiven; God has put His righteousness on your book, and He is not keeping a record of your sins.

## Don't Record Others' Sins

Third, *don't keep a record of other people's sins.* First Corinthians 13:5 reminds us that love does not keep a record of wrongs. Don't keep in your mind and heart a record of the bad things people have done to you. Just turn it over to God. God is not keeping a record; why should you? Just lovingly forgive them.

## God Records Our Works

Finally, *remember that God is keeping a record of our works.* He has given us righteousness that we might live righteous lives. Righteousness is not only *imputed* (put on our account), but through the Holy Spirit righteousness is *imparted.* Let's be faithful. Let's rejoice at this wonderful freedom that we have. We do not have this debt hanging over our head. We have been forgiven. We have a record that is clean. The righteousness of Jesus Christ has been put to our account.

It is no wonder that David said, "Blessed is he whose iniquities are forgiven and whose sins are covered. Blessed is the man to whom the Lord will not impute sin" (see Ps. 32:1,2). God has written His righteousness on your record; now let Him write that righteousness on your life.

## Chapter 8

# Sanctification: Holiness and Obedience

Sanctification is the gracious work of God in setting the believer apart for Himself and for service in the world. Sanctification has three aspects to it. The theologians call this *positional* sanctification, *practical,* or *progressive,* sanctification and *perfect* sanctification.

## Positional Sanctification

*Positional* sanctification means that, in Christ, we have been set apart to belong to God and to serve Him. Positional sanctification never changes. First Corinthians 1:2 says, "Unto the church of God which is at Corinth, to them that are sanctified in Christ Jesus, called to be saints, with all that in every place call upon the name of Jesus Christ our Lord, both their's and our's."

You can hardly call the people in the church at Corinth godly people. Some of them were getting drunk; some of them were living in immorality; some of them were suing each other. And yet Paul addressed them as a church (called-out people), *sanctified* in Christ Jesus. That is positional sanctification; it never changes.

## Practical, or Progressive, Sanctification

*Practical, or progressive,* sanctification has to do with our everyday life. Our Lord Jesus prayed, "Sanctify them through thy truth: thy word is truth" (John 17:17). Since we have a holy position in Christ, we should live like it.

## Perfect Sanctification

*Perfect* sanctification, of course, will take place when we see the Lord Jesus Christ at His coming, and we shall be like Him, "for we shall see him as he is" (I John 3:2). These three aspects of sanctification relate to each other. Because we know we have been set apart by God and because we know that Jesus is coming and we shall be like Him, we want to keep our lives clean today. We want to seek to become more like the Lord Jesus Christ.

One theologian said, "It is one thing for sin to live in us; another for us to live in sin." We can't help the fact that our old nature is a sinful nature. But God has given us a new nature, and this new nature enables us to live a holy life. We are talking about practical, or progressive, sanctification—day by day becoming more like the Saviour, day by day overcoming sin and temptation, day by day growing stronger in spiritual things.

I want to focus on II Corinthians 7:1: "Having therefore these promises, dearly beloved, let us cleanse ourselves from all filthiness of the flesh and

65

spirit, perfecting holiness in the fear of God." In this verse we have a series of dual truths. If we understand these truths, it will help us in our progressive sanctification.

## Two Aspects of Sin

To begin with, Paul pointed out that there are *two different aspects to sin:* There are sins of the flesh and there are sins of the spirit. "Let us cleanse ourselves from all filthiness of the flesh and spirit" (II Cor. 7:1). In other words, we have here the Prodigal Son (he was guilty of sins of the flesh) and the elder brother (he was guilty of sins of the spirit). When David committed adultery with Bathsheba, that was a sin of the flesh. When David numbered the people in pride and rebelled against God, that was a sin of the spirit. There are sins of action, and there are sins of attitude.

### Sins of the Flesh

Let's talk about these sins of the flesh. By the flesh, of course, Paul meant the old nature. When you and I were born again, God gave us a new nature, but He did not change the old nature. You and I are capable of sinning today. We don't *want* to, because the desires of the new nature have lifted us higher. But now we see what sin is really like. The Word of God and the Spirit of God have revealed to us the awfulness of sin, and we want nothing to do with it. But we are capable of sinning.

Everything the Bible has to say about the flesh is negative. "It is the Spirit who gives life," said the

66

Lord Jesus, "the flesh profits nothing" (see John 6:63). We are to have no confidence in the flesh (see Phil. 3:3). The flesh is that which produces sin. Out of the heart of man (the old nature) comes all sorts of evil things—lying and lust and all the things that wreck our lives and ruin our testimonies. Galatians 5:19-21 has recorded the works of the flesh, and 17 different sins are mentioned there. In Romans 1:23 different sins are mentioned. The flesh is very productive when it comes to producing sin, and the flesh cannot be changed. There are sins of the flesh, and we need to wash ourselves, or cleanse ourselves, from all filthiness of the flesh.

## Sins of the Spirit

There are also sins of the spirit. You and I may not be guilty of drunkenness, adultery, gluttony or laziness, but how about pride, stubbornness or criticism? G. Campbell Morgan used to call the sins of the spirit "sins in good standing." You have to be careful about them. You may not be a Prodigal Son, but you might be an elder brother—so critical that you won't fellowship with your brother. There are two aspects of sin, and we have to deal with them— the filthiness of the flesh and also the filthiness of the spirit.

## Two Aspects of Holiness

Second Corinthians 7:1 reveals that there are also *two aspects to holiness*. There is a negative aspect and a positive aspect. Negatively, "let us cleanse ourselves." Positively, "perfecting holiness in the fear of God."

## Cleansing

"Let us cleanse ourselves" means *once and for all* let us cleanse out of our lives the defilement of sin. In fact, Paul wrote about this in II Corinthians 6:14-18. "Be ye not unequally yoked together with unbelievers" (v. 14). This is a farm picture. You don't yoke an ox and an ass together. They have two different temperaments, and they are not going to be able to work together. Believers should not be yoked together with unbelievers in marriage or in business.

"For what fellowship hath righteousness with unrighteousness?" (v. 14). The word "fellowship" is a *commercial* term—it means partnership. Righteousness cannot be in partnership with unrighteousness. "What communion hath light with darkness?" (v. 14). The word "communion" means *to have in common.* It is a family term. We do not have anything in common with unsaved people other than our humanity, because we are light and they are darkness. We have righteousness and they have unrighteousness.

"What concord hath Christ with Belial [Satan]?" (v. 15). The word "concord" here is a musical term—it means "symphony," it has to do with harmony. We aren't even playing in the same orchestra with the unsaved! We aren't following the same conductor or reading the same score. Therefore, how can we ever make music together? It is such a sad thing when believers try to manufacture harmony with unbelievers. You can't make a beautiful home that way.

"Or what part [real estate term, meaning a part of land] hath he that believeth with an infidel [an unbeliever]? What agreement [political term, meaning voting together] hath the temple of God with idols? for ye are the temple of the living God; as God hath said, I will dwell in them, and walk in them; and I will be their God, and they shall be my people" (vv. 15,16).

So the first aspect of holiness is to cleanse ourselves. This doesn't mean we become isolationists. We have to live *in* the world but not *like* the world. We are to be the salt of the earth and the light of the world; we have to have contact but not contamination. This is what the Bible calls separation—setting ourselves apart and saying, "I am not going to vote with unbelievers. I don't agree with them. I am not going to try to make music with unbelievers, because I just don't have the same conductor that they have." Separation, not isolation, not insulation, but biblical separation means cleansing ourselves.

Often we pray, "O God, cleanse me." And God comes back and says, "Why don't you cleanse yourself? Get those records out of your record library. Get those books and magazines out of your library. Why don't you cleanse yourself? Put away these things and be separate." Isaiah 1:16 says, "Wash you, make you clean."

### Living in His Presence

The positive follows: "Perfecting holiness in the fear of God" (II Cor. 7:1). It isn't enough to be

69

negative like the Pharisees and *not* do certain things. We have to be positive. We have here a consistent, constant process. Holiness is what God is, and as we grow in holiness, we become more like God.

In the Old Testament tabernacle there was a laver. The laver made cleansing possible. That's negative. But there was also a Holy of Holies. The priest was only allowed to enter there once a year. You and I can enter into God's presence at any time. In fact, we should *live* in His presence. The laver cleanses us, but being in fellowship with God in the Holy of Holies perfects us. Don't be afraid of holiness. Holiness is not this "brittle piety" that some people manifest—a religiosity that is so artificial. No, holiness is *wholeness*. Holiness is to your soul what health is to your body. There are two aspects to sin—sins of the flesh and sins of the spirit. And there are two aspects to holiness—cleansing ourselves and perfecting holiness.

## Two Aspects of Obedience

Finally, there are two aspects of *obedience*— two motivations in this verse.

### Love of God

Why should we cleanse ourselves? Why should we perfect holiness? Because of *God's love*. "Having therefore these promises, dearly beloved" (II Cor. 7:1). What promises? "Wherefore come out from among them, and be ye separate, saith the Lord, and touch not the unclean thing; and I will receive you, and will be a Father unto you, and ye shall be my sons and daughters, saith the Lord Almighty" (6:17,18). Notice the promises here.

When you were saved, God became your Father. But He cannot *be* a Father to you if you are disobedient. We parents long to love our children and share the very best with them, but sometimes they won't let us. So the promise is given that God will receive us into a deeper fellowship if we are obedient. He will be a Father to us, and we will be His sons and daughters. Not only is His *love* available to us, but His *power* is also available to us, for He is the Lord Almighty. He promises to receive us. He promises to bless us. He promises a deeper fellowship with Him through the Word of God and through the Holy Spirit.

Listen to John 14:21-23: "He that hath my commandments, and keepeth them, he it is that loveth me: and he that loveth me shall be loved of my Father, and I will love him, and will manifest myself to him. Judas saith unto him, not Iscariot, Lord, how is it that thou wilt manifest thyself unto us, and not unto the world? Jesus answered and said unto him, If a man love me, he will keep my words: and my Father will love him, and we will come unto him, and make our abode with him." That is a deeper fellowship with God, because we are cleansing ourselves and perfecting holiness in the fear of God.

### Fear of God

The first aspect of obedience is love; the second is *fear*—"perfecting holiness in the fear of God"

71

(II Cor. 7:1). We don't have just God's promises; we also have God's discipline. If we do not walk in separation, God has to discipline us. He does not want us to become prisoners; He wants us to be sons and daughters who walk with Him. He says, "Come out, be separate, touch not the unclean thing, and I will be a Father to you" (see 6:17). We do this in the fear of God.

There is a sweet, deep fellowship with God that is so precious. There is also a walk with God that demands fear and reverence. We ought to reverence our Father in heaven because it is He who has commanded us to be holy. This is practical, progressive sanctification—being aware of the sins of the flesh and of the spirit, being diligent to cleanse ourselves and perfect holiness. We are being motivated by the love of God because of His promises and by the fear of God because of His discipline. "Having therefore these promises, dearly beloved, let us cleanse ourselves from all filthiness of the flesh and spirit, perfecting holiness in the fear of God."

Chapter 9

# Reconciliation: "Bring Us Together"

During the 1968 presidential campaign, the town of Deshler, Ohio, became famous. One of the candidates was making a whistle-stop there. A 13-year-old girl picked up a sign that someone had dropped and held it up. The sign said, "Bring us together again." The news media picked this up, and the girl in Deshler, Ohio, became famous overnight.

"Bring us together again"—that's the cry of hearts today. There is a need for reconciliation, for people to be brought back together again.

The Bible begins with a record of perfect harmony—heaven and earth working together in joyful cooperation. But then sin enters into the picture and there is division, dissention, death and separation. Man is separated from God. Man runs from God and hides. And then man is separated from man with brother killing brother. There is a separation of races and nations as Genesis records the awful consequences of sin. The great need is for reconciliation, and that is the work of our Lord Jesus Christ.

Reconciliation means to bring together that which

was separated or at war. Reconciliation involves the sinner, the Saviour and the believer.

## The Sinner

Reconciliation implies that the sinner is at war with God. Second Corinthians 5:17-21 says, "Therefore if any man be in Christ, he is a new creature: old things are passed away; behold, all things are become new. And all things are of God, who hath reconciled us to himself by Jesus Christ, and hath given to us the ministry of reconciliation; to wit, that God was in Christ, reconciling the world unto himself, not imputing their trespasses unto them: and hath committed unto us the word of reconciliation. Now then we are ambassadors for Christ, as though God did beseech you by us: we pray [beg] you in Christ's stead, be ye reconciled to God. For he hath made him to be sin for us, who knew no sin; that we might be made the righteousness of God in him."

Romans 5:7-10 says, "For scarcely for a righteous man will one die: yet peradventure for a good man some would even dare to die. But God commendeth his love toward us, in that, while we were yet sinners, Christ died for us. Much more then, being now justified by his blood, we shall be saved from wrath through him. For if, when we were enemies, we were reconciled to God by the death of his Son, much more, being reconciled, we shall be saved by his life."

Rome had two kinds of provinces—senatorial provinces and imperial provinces. What was the difference? The senatorial provinces were peaceful, and Rome did not put any troops there. The imperial provinces were the warlike provinces where there was trouble. Emperor Augustus ruled those provinces directly through his troops, and he always sent ambassadors to those provinces. The fact that God has chosen Christians to be His ambassadors in this world is an indication that the world is an imperial province at war with God.

Many people dispute this fact. They say that man is basically good. After all, not everybody is in jail, not everybody has broken the law. But the problem is, people look only on the surface; God sees the heart. Most people look only at actions and ignore motives. God sees the pride and rebellion in the human heart. The enmity between sinners and God is serious. By nature the sinner is at enmity with God. If you have never been born again, then you are at war with God. "In my flesh, dwelleth no good thing" (Rom. 7:18). "The heart is deceitful above all things, and desperately wicked" (Jer. 17:9). By *nature* the sinner is at enmity with God, and by *action* the sinner is at enmity with God.

Isaiah 53:6 says, "All we like sheep have gone astray; we have turned every one to his own way." The fact that man today looks up and says no to God is evidence that man is at enmity with God. Man lives for the world and the flesh; his motive is self-glory. He is interested only in pleasing himself; he is not interested in glorifying God. The Word of God tells us that friendship with the world is enmity with God (see James 4:4); and of course, the un-

75

saved person lives for the world and the things of the world.

More than that, the unsaved person so often brags about his own self-righteousness. "The carnal mind is enmity against God" (Rom. 8:7). Men boast of their own goodness! So the sinner is at war with God, and if he stays at war with God, he will die and be separated from God throughout all eternity.

### The Saviour

This is where reconciliation comes in. The Saviour is the second Person involved in the work of reconciliation. He loves and reconciles lost sinners. God did not need to be reconciled to man. It was Adam who ran from God, not God who ran from Adam. When man sinned against God, God went and sought man. God called to Adam, "Where art thou?" (Gen. 3:9). God never forsakes man. This is very important to remember. If God were to forsake you for an instant, you would die, for "in him we live, and move, and have our being" (Acts 17:28). So God did not need to be reconciled to man; it is man who needs to be reconciled to God.

This is why God sent His Son, the Lord Jesus Christ. "But God commendeth his love toward us, in that, while we were yet sinners, Christ died for us" (Rom. 5:8). The word "commendeth" means "proved." God *proved* His love toward us. The proof of God's love is not seen in nature or in history, although we can see Him there. The proof is at Calvary, on the cross where Christ died for our sins.

God hates our sins, but God loves the sinner. The more you love someone, the more you despise the bad things that they do. Every parent knows this. You love your son, you love your daughter, but you hate the things they are doing that are wrecking their lives. God loves lost sinners, and the more sinners rebel against God, the more they are sinning against the love of God. This is why the Saviour came to die.

## Obstacles to Reconciliation

There are some obstacles to reconciliation. In our human life we may reconcile people who are at war with each other and not really solve the problem. Some reconciliation is only a truce, and it doesn't last. God doesn't do His work that way. God is concerned with removing the obstacles which stand between Him and the sinner whom God loves.

Of course, the first obstacle is God's holy Law. God cannot break His own Law. "The soul that sinneth, it shall die" (Ezek. 18:4). "Ye shall be holy; for I am holy" (Lev. 11:44). God's holy Law stands between the sinner and heaven.

Second, there is man's guilt. God just can't take the record He has of man's guilt and destroy it. God knows what is going on. He watches, and He judges. Nothing can be hidden from His eyes. You may think you are hiding something from God, but God knows all about it. God's holy Law stands between the sinner and God. Man's guilt stands between the sinner and God. And more than that,

77

*man's very selfish nature stands between the sinner and God.* At heart we are rebels. If there is going to be reconciliation, God has to do something about His Law, about man's guilt and about man's selfish, sinful nature.

Of course, man tries to do this himself, doesn't he? Man lowers the standards and says, "Well, I'm as good as anybody else." Man says, "Well, my guilt is not too bad. I'll just start all over again." But even if we did start all over again today, what about our past record of guilt? Man cannot change his own heart. That heart can be changed only by God.

### Removal of the Obstacles

Jesus Christ removed all of these obstacles. He satisfied the holy demands of God's Law. We have already discussed this in our study of propitiation. When our Lord died on the cross, He met the demands of God's holy Law.

Second, He bore the guilt of our sins on the cross. This is justification. In other words, we can stand before God in the righteousness of Christ. There is no more guilt.

Third, because of His death, burial and resurrection, Jesus Christ can change the heart. He can give us, not only a new *position* but a new *disposition*. The Bible calls this regeneration, being born again. "The love of God is shed abroad in our hearts by the Holy Ghost" (Rom. 5:5).

So Jesus Christ has reconciled God and man. He has removed the obstacles. The Law has been satisfied, the guilt has been paid for, and the heart can be changed through the power of Jesus Christ. Of course, the price for all of this was His death on the cross. "For he hath made him to be sin for us, who knew no sin; that we might be made the righteousness of God in him" (II Cor. 5:21). Reconciliation is not man's work, it is God's work. It is God who brings us together through Jesus Christ.

### The Believer

Now let us look at the believer. What does it mean to us as believers to be reconciled? Why would an unbeliever even want to be reconciled?

Let me make it very clear that reconciliation is not merely a second chance. If it were only a second chance, then the next time you sinned, you would be lost. Reconciliation is not a temporary truce. God doesn't change, God doesn't lie. What God does, He does permanently. Reconciliation is a permanent bringing together of the believing sinner and God through Jesus Christ.

I would remind you that the cross is a plus sign, and a plus sign brings things together. Now the argument in Romans 5 is simply this: If, when we were God's enemies, He reconciled us through Christ, how much more will He bless us now that we are reconciled? Romans 5:10 says, "For if, when we were enemies, we were reconciled to God by the death of his Son, much more, being reconciled, we shall be saved by his life." Romans 5 uses the phrase "much more" several times. Reconciliation gives you "much more."

Now that we are His children, we have security.

We are justified by His blood. Nothing can change that. We have victory. We can "reign in life through Jesus Christ" (see v. 17). If He did so much for us by His death, *how much more* He can do for us in His life. We are not only saved by His death, but we are also saved by His life. Saved from what? Saved from defeat, saved from future wrath. "Much more then, being now justified by his blood, we shall be saved from wrath through him" (v. 9). So we have security, we have victory, we have sufficiency. All that we need God gives to us. Romans 5:21 says, "That as sin hath reigned unto death, even so might grace reign through righteousness unto eternal life by Jesus Christ our Lord." God takes rebels and makes kings out of them. God takes slaves and makes sovereigns out of them. That is reconciliation.

Along with this comes responsibility. We are ambassadors for Christ. The world we live in is at war with God. Sinners need to be reconciled to God. God is already reconciled—God has turned His face toward us. Now it is our task to spread the Good News, to tell people they don't have to be at war with God because God is not at war with them.

This is a day of God's grace. There is coming a Day of Judgment, and then it will be too late. What a privilege it is to be an ambassador for Jesus Christ—wherever you are—at home, in your neighborhood, at work, at school. What good news we have—the Good News of reconciliation.

Chapter 10

# Redemption: Set Free From Bondage

Freedom is a very precious commodity in today's world. Each year more and more people lose their personal freedom. An organization called Freedom House monitors this situation, and they now report that only 36 percent of the world's population is truly free.

Freedom was a very precious commodity in the New Testament world. One specialist tells us there were at least 60 million slaves in the Roman Empire. Ancient society was built on the foundation of slavery. There were, at one time, nearly half a million slaves in the city of Corinth alone. And so the word "redemption" brought great joy and hope to these people.

Redemption is a key word in the Bible and a key word in the Christian life. It means *to purchase and set free by paying a price.* That payment, of course, was the blood of Jesus Christ. "In whom we have redemption through his blood" (Eph. 1:7). Jesus died on the cross that we might be redeemed. He purchased us and set us free by paying a price.

From what kind of bondage have we been freed because we have trusted Christ as our Saviour?

There are at least four different kinds of bondage from which we have been set free, and we want to examine them.

## Bondage to Sin

First of all, we are freed from bondage to sin. Titus 2:11-14: "For the grace of God that bringeth salvation hath appeared to all men, teaching us that, denying ungodliness and worldly lusts, we should live soberly, righteously, and godly, in this present world [age]; looking for that blessed hope, and the glorious appearing of the great God and our Saviour Jesus Christ; who gave himself for us, that he might redeem us from all iniquity, and purify unto himself a peculiar people, zealous of good works." We have been redeemed from bondage to sin.

This, of course, reminds us of Israel in Egypt. They were in bondage in Egypt. They had to answer to taskmasters. Day after day they were slaving and not being paid for it. Day after day they labored and were mistreated. It was terrible bondage.

You can't convince unsaved people that they are in bondage because they think they are free. This is a part of the deceitfulness of sin. Sin promises freedom but always brings slavery. Sin promises joy and ultimately brings pain. Sin promises success, but ultimately it brings failure. The Prodigal Son wanted to be free. He wanted to get away from his big brother and his father, so he went out into a far country. He thought he was free, but he discovered his freedom soon turned into bondage. He became a slave, not only of a Gentile taskmaster, but he became a servant of the pigs.

You and I, before we were saved, were not in much better shape. Titus 3:3 says, "For we ourselves also were sometimes [once] foolish, disobedient, deceived, serving divers [various] lusts and pleasures, living in malice and envy, hateful, and hating one another." That doesn't sound like freedom, does it?

But when God's grace appeared in Jesus Christ, we were set free. It was nothing we did ourselves; He did it for us. Titus 3:4,5 says, "But after that the kindness and love of God our Saviour toward man appeared, not by works of righteousness which we have done, but according to his mercy he saved us." We have been redeemed from bondage to sin, and this redemption leads to reformation. Not only do we have freedom from the guilt and the penalty of sin, but we also have freedom *not to sin,* through the power of the Holy Spirit. We have a blessed new hope: "Looking for that blessed hope, and the glorious appearing of the great God and our Saviour Jesus Christ" (2:13).

Have you been set free, or redeemed, from bondage to sin?

### Bondage to the Old Life

The second kind of bondage from which we have been redeemed is bondage to the old life. First Peter 1:18,19 says, "Forasmuch as ye know that ye were not redeemed with corruptible things, as silver and gold, from your vain conversation [manner of life] received by tradition from your fathers; but with the precious blood of Christ, as of a lamb without blemish and without spot." The blood of Jesus Christ has set us free from bondage to the old life.

It is interesting the way Peter described this old life: "Your vain conversation [manner of life] received by tradition from your fathers." Vain means empty, the vanity of sin. In I Peter 4:2-4, Peter described this further: "That he [the believer] no longer should live the rest of his time in the flesh to the lusts of men, but to the will of God. For the time past of our life may suffice us to have wrought the will of the Gentiles, when we walked in lasciviousness, lusts, excess of wine, revellings, banquetings [carousings], and abominable idolatries: wherein they think it strange that ye run not with them to the same excess of riot, speaking evil of you."

The life we used to live was a life of vanity. We thought it was a life of pleasure! Unsaved people sometimes say, "Oh, you Christians don't know what it is to really enjoy life! I am free! I am doing my thing!" The Bible describes what you are doing: "Lasciviousness, lusts, excess of wine, revellings, banquetings [carousings], and abominable idolatries"—a flood of dissipation (v. 3). This doesn't sound like freedom to me. The sad thing is that many people think because they are doing their own thing they are free, when true freedom is doing the will of God.

People have the idea that the will of God is bondage. It is not bondage; the will of God is beautiful freedom. When the Lord Jesus Christ saves us, He saves us and redeems us from bondage to the old life. We must not live the rest of our lives the way we used to live.

How long will the rest of our lives be? We don't know, nobody knows. We may have many years, we may have many days. We don't know. We could be called home to glory before the day ends. We don't know. "It is appointed unto men once to die, but after this the judgment" (Heb. 9:27). It is an appointment, not an accident, and God knows when it is going to be.

When you are redeemed, you are set free from bondage to the old life. This is why Ephesians 5:16 tells us to redeem the time. Don't live the rest of your life the way you used to live. You have been set free from that. "Old things are passed away; behold, all things are become new" (II Cor. 5:17). Therefore, redeem the time, buy up the opportunity, make the most of the rest of your life.

I would like to apply that, if I may. Perhaps you are born again, but you are following the traditions of other people. You are doing what everybody else does. Why don't you ask God what *He* wants you to do with the rest of your life? Perhaps you are in the wrong school, and you ought to be in another school training to serve God. Perhaps you are pursuing the wrong career. Perhaps you are a businessman, and somewhat successful, but God is calling you into His service. You could use your experience and your gifts to glorify God in full-time Christian service. If you knew you had only ten years left to live or one year left to live, how would this change your life? We should be living each day as though it were our last. We are redeemed from bondage to sin; we are redeemed from bondage to the old life. We should live wholly for God.

## Bondage to the Law

We are also redeemed from bondage to the Law. Galatians 3:13 says, "Christ hath redeemed us from the curse of the law, being made a curse for us: for it is written, Cursed is every one that hangeth on a tree." Galatians 4:4,5 says, "But when the fulness of the time was come, God sent forth his Son, made of a woman, made under the law, to redeem them that were under the law, that we might receive the adoption of sons."

The Law was never given to save anybody; the Law was given to reveal sin. The Law is a mirror. You don't wash your face in the mirror; you examine your face in the mirror. If you discover your face is dirty, then you need to wash your face. When you and I look into God's holy Law, we see how sinful we are, and the Law pronounces a curse. Galatians 3:10 says, "For as many as are of the works of the law are under the curse: for it is written, Cursed is every one that continueth not in all things which are written in the book of the law to do them."

There are two very important facts in this verse. Number one, if you are going to be saved by Law, you have to keep *all* of it. You can't pick and choose. It is not *a la carte*. God puts the meal in front of you and says, "This is it! You have to obey all of the Law. You can't pick and choose."

Second, you have to *continue* to obey it. If once

86

you disobey, you are under a curse. The Word of God makes it very clear that the Law brings condemnation, not salvation. The Old Testament Jew was under Law; he had to keep certain days as special days. He had to avoid certain foods and certain places. He had to go through certain ceremonial rituals. We have been redeemed from the Law and from the curse of the Law. Galatians 5:1 says, "Stand fast therefore in the liberty wherewith Christ hath made us free."

This does not make us lawless. The Law of God is written in our hearts by the Holy Spirit. We obey God's Law because we love God. We obey God's Law because our new nature impels us to obey God's Law. The old nature *knows* no Law; the new nature *needs* no Law. There never was a Law given that could change or control the old nature. Jesus Christ has redeemed us from the curse of the Law. "There is therefore now no condemnation to them which are in Christ Jesus" (Rom. 8:1).

### Bondage to Bodies of Sin

We are also redeemed from bondage to our bodies of sin. This hasn't happened yet, but it is going to happen. In Romans 8:23 we read: "[We are] waiting for the adoption, to wit [that is], the redemption of our body." Ephesians 1:13, 14 tells us that the Holy Spirit has sealed us unto the day of redemption. Ephesians 4:30 says, "Grieve not the holy Spirit of God, whereby ye are sealed unto the day of redemption." There is coming a day of redemption.

Today our spirits have been redeemed, but our bodies have not been redeemed. Our bodies are still subject to sickness and pain, accident and illness. Our bodies still experience decay. But one day we are going to see Jesus Christ and have glorified bodies. "Our conversation [citizenship] is in heaven; from whence also we look for the Saviour, the Lord Jesus Christ: who shall change our vile body, that it may be fashioned like unto his glorious body" (Phil. 3:20,21). We are looking forward to a glorious day of redemption.

Jesus Christ has redeemed us from sin. He has redeemed us from the old life. He has redeemed us from the Law. And He will one day come and redeem us from these bodies of sin that create so much trouble for us.

This redemption that we have is not temporary. The word "redemption" means to purchase out of the slave market and set free, *never to become a slave again.* A man could purchase a slave and *keep* him a slave. Jesus didn't do that. Our Lord Jesus has purchased us by His blood and set us free to glorify Him.

Hebrews 9:12 tells us that Jesus Christ is the author of eternal redemption. How long are we redeemed? For eternity. It is *eternal* redemption. We have been delivered from the power of darkness, we have been translated into the kingdom of God's dear Son (Col. 1:13,14). If you are redeemed through faith in Christ, rejoice. Rejoice in your freedom in Christ, and use that freedom to serve others and glorify the Lord Jesus Christ.

Chapter 11

# Intercession: Caring and Praying

Loneliness is becoming a real problem today in spite of the population explosion and in spite of all the media available. Loneliness is that feeling deep down inside that nobody thinks about you or cares about you. Loneliness is not the same as solitude. Solitude is good for us; it helps to build us up. Even our Lord Jesus Christ came apart from the crowd and enjoyed fellowship with God in solitude. Loneliness tears us down. Loneliness is that awful feeling down inside that you don't count and that if you were missing nobody really would miss you. Henry David Thoreau, the naturalist, defined city life as millions of people being lonely together. Of course, the result of all of this is often physical illness, emotional problems, spiritual problems, sometimes rebellion, sometimes withdrawal, sometimes even suicide.

The wonderful message of the Gospel is that the Father cares for us and that Jesus cares. We as believers ought to care. This is where intercession comes in. The truth of intercession proves that God is for us and we need not feel alone or afraid. To intercede means to act between parties so as to bring them together, and togetherness is the opposite of loneliness.

I would like to discuss with you a threefold intercession that is found in the Bible. And if you and I will understand this threefold intercession, we can never really be lonely again.

### Jesus Cares and Intercedes

First of all, *Jesus cares and intercedes for us.* Romans 8:34 says, "Who is he that condemneth? It is Christ that died, yea rather, that is risen again, who is even at the right hand of God, who also maketh intercession for us." The Lord Jesus Christ today in heaven is interceding for His people. When He was here on earth, He had a prayer life that touched the lives of many people. In fact, when He was dying on the cross, He prayed, "Father, forgive them; for they know not what they do" (Luke 23:34). The Prophet Isaiah prophesied that Jesus Christ would make intercession for the transgressors (see Isa. 53:12), and He did.

Today the Lord Jesus Christ is not praying for a lost world. That comes as a surprise to some people, but it is true. "I pray not for the world," He said in John 17:9. Rather, He is praying for His own in heaven, and He is interceding for us in a twofold way—as our Advocate and as our High Priest.

The ministry of our Lord Jesus Christ in heaven as the Advocate is described in I John 2:1: "My little children, these things write I unto you, that ye sin not. And if any man sin, we have an advocate with the Father, Jesus Christ the righteous."

The word translated "advocate" means a counsel for the defense. It means one who lends his presence to his friends. The Lord Jesus Christ in heaven represents us before the throne of God. This does not mean that God the Father is against us. It simply means that we ourselves cannot approach a holy God in our own name or with our own merits. We come through the merits of Jesus Christ.

As our Advocate, the Lord Jesus Christ restores us when we have sinned. It is true that we shouldn't sin, but we do. Each of us faces temptation, and sometimes we fall. John said, "Get up, confess that sin, and your Advocate will restore you." "If we confess our sins, he is faithful and just to forgive us our sins, and to cleanse us from all unrighteousness" (I John 1:9).

But as our High Priest, the Lord Jesus Christ intercedes *to keep us from sinning*. It really isn't necessary for us to sin. When we are tempted, we can come to our Heavenly Intercessor, our High Priest, and He can give us the strength and grace that we need. "Seeing then that we have a great high priest, that is passed into the heavens, Jesus the Son of God, let us hold fast our profession. For we have not an high priest which cannot be touched with the feeling of our infirmities; but was in all points tempted like as we are, yet without sin. Let us therefore come boldly unto the throne of grace, that we may obtain mercy, and find grace to help in time of need" (Heb. 4:14-16). Our Lord Jesus Christ cares and intercedes for us in heaven.

He knows our weaknesses, and He knows our temptations. Jesus Christ has suffered every kind of testing you and I will ever face. In fact, He endured far more, because He was perfect. You and I do not have the kind of sensitivity that He had when He was here on earth, living in a perfect body. Jesus Christ has been through fires that we will never see. He has carried burdens that we will never feel, and He has succeeded. In heaven today He prays for us, He intercedes for us, and therefore He is able to help us succeed.

Hebrews 7:25 says, "Wherefore he is able also to save them to the uttermost that come unto God by him, seeing he ever liveth to make intercession for them." We are saved eternally, we have security, because Jesus is ever living to represent us in heaven. Jesus cares and intercedes.

### The Holy Spirit Cares and Intercedes

Second, *the Holy Spirit cares and intercedes.* Romans 8:26 says, "Likewise the Spirit also helpeth our infirmities." What is our infirmity? "For we know not what we should pray for as we ought: but the Spirit itself maketh intercession for us with groanings which cannot be uttered. And he that searcheth the hearts knoweth what is the mind of the Spirit, because he maketh intercession for the saints according to the will of God" (vv. 26,27).

The Holy Spirit dwells within the body of each believer. Romans 8:9 tells us very clearly that unless we have the Holy Spirit we are not saved: "Now if any man have not the Spirit of Christ, he is none of his." The Holy Spirit lives in us, and He intercedes for us. The Holy Spirit knows the mind of the Father. A beautiful relationship is described here. The Holy Spirit intercedes for us on earth, and Jesus Christ intercedes for us in heaven. Is it any wonder that the Devil attacks us? And the greatest wonder of all is that we should fall when we have this kind of assistance to see us through to victory.

Jude 1:20 tells us we should be praying in the Holy Spirit. I believe the biblical pattern for prayer is that we pray to the Father, through the Son, in the Holy Spirit. Many times in your praying the Spirit of God will guide you to pray about something. I have been awakened at night or early in the morning with an impression upon my mind and heart that I should pray about something. And so I have prayed about it. Then I tried to remember when that time was, and I have checked afterward, and I have often discovered that the person for whom I was praying was going through a difficult time.

I'm sure people have been stirred by the Spirit to pray for me. It's a marvelous thing to share in the intercessory work of the Holy Spirit, for the Spirit helps us to pray in the will of God. "We know that all things work together for good to them that love God, to them who are the called according to his purpose" (Rom. 8:28). As the Holy Spirit directs us, we fulfill the purpose of God.

## Believers Should Care and Intercede

Third, *you and I as believers should care and intercede.* "I exhort therefore, that, first of all, supplications, prayers, intercessions, and giving of thanks, be made for all men; for kings, and for all that are in authority; that we may lead a quiet and peaceable life in all godliness and honesty. For this is good and acceptable in the sight of God our Saviour; who will have all men to be saved, and to come unto the knowledge of the truth" (I Tim. 2:1-4). Verse 8 says, "I will therefore that men pray every where, lifting up holy hands, without wrath and doubting."

In the Bible you find a number of great people who were intercessors who stood between God and man and prayed. Abraham was a great intercessor. Had it not been for Abraham's praying, Lot would never have been delivered from Sodom. Abraham knew how to intercede.

Moses was a great intercessor. Moses met God on the mountaintop and interceded for the Children of Israel. In fact, he offered himself to die on their behalf.

Daniel was a great man of intercession, and so were Ezra and Nehemiah. So was the Apostle Paul. Paul said his heart was just breaking because of the needs of his people, the Israelites. So when you intercede, you are a part of a great company of people; and of course, the greatest of all was our Lord Jesus Christ.

For whom should we pray? For all men, and that

covers a lot of people! We should pray for those who are sick and for those who are well, for those who have problems and for those who don't have problems. We must pray for the saved and the unsaved. We should pray "for all that are in authority" (v. 2). Pray for the president, for the governor of your state, for the mayor, for those who are in places of leadership. For what purpose? "That we may lead a quiet and peaceable life in all godliness and honesty" (v. 2). I really believe that if Christians were interceding more for people in public life, it would be safer on the streets and we would have better enforcement of the laws. We are to intercede for people in authority.

Certainly we are supposed to intercede for those who are lost, for God "will have all men to be saved" (v. 4). I have heard people say, "We aren't told to pray for lost sinners." I think we are. I think if God wants *all men* to be saved and come to the knowledge of the truth and we are supposed to pray for *all men*, then we ought to pray for the lost. Do you have a list of names of lost people for whom you pray?

Of course, we have to have the right conditions in our own life. First Timothy 2:8 says, "I will therefore that men pray every where, lifting up holy hands, without wrath and doubting." This means that we will be living a pure life, a life of fellowship and love, a life without dissension. We should be peace-loving people; we should be peacemakers, not troublemakers. We should have clean hands and a pure

95

heart, and we should be interceding in the will of God.

Intercession is a tremendous privilege. I trust that each day you get alone with God and have before you the Word of God and perhaps a list of people about whom you are concerned. The interesting thing is this: You cannot pray for people very much without getting interested in them and learning to love them and wanting to do something for them. Prayer is really dangerous, because the more you pray, the more you are going to get involved. One of the best ways to cure loneliness is to pray and to get involved.

I trust you are praying for the pastor of your church, for your Sunday school teachers and for the spiritual leaders in your church. I trust that God is using you to intercede. Jesus cares and intercedes. As our Advocate, He restores us, and as our High Priest, He strengthens us to keep us from sinning. The Holy Spirit cares and intercedes. He guides us in the will of God and helps us to pray in the will of God as we surrender to Him. And you and I should care and intercede.

Don't ever say to somebody, "Well, the least I can do is pray for you." My friend, the *most* you can do is pray, because intercession has great power, and intercession is a great privilege.

Chapter 12

# Mediation: Settling Enmity

"For there is one God, and one mediator between God and men, the man Christ Jesus" (I Tim. 2:5). In these days of international conferences and labor problems, we frequently hear the word "mediation." A mediator is someone who seeks to bring two or more opposing parties together in some kind of agreement.

In the New Testament world, a mediator was a neutral party that both sides could trust—an umpire or a negotiator who would not only establish peaceful relationships between the parties but also guarantee the terms of the agreement. First Timothy 2:5 tells us that Jesus Christ is a Mediator. You will notice that "mediation" is found in the context of the doctrine of intercession because intercession and mediation go together.

What is mediation? Mediation is the ministry of Jesus Christ in bringing God and man together and settling the enmity once and for all. First Timothy 2:6 says, "Who gave himself a ransom for all, to be testified in due time."

## A Qualified Mediator

Is He qualified to be a mediator? He certainly is.

### Qualified in His Person

To begin with, He is qualified in His Person. He is both God and man which is important. A mediator must be able to understand both parties. Jesus Christ in His Person is a perfect mediator because He is God and He is man. "There is one God, and one mediator between God and men, the man Christ Jesus" (I Tim. 2:5). But this man Christ Jesus is also God.

It never ceases to amaze me how people can read the New Testament and come to the conclusion that Jesus is not God. The demons announced that He was God. He Himself claimed to be God. In fact, when He was under oath in the Jewish court, He said that He was God. The entire Bible bears witness to the fact that Jesus Christ is God.

When He came to earth, Jesus became man—sinless man, sympathetic man. When He was here on earth, our Lord Jesus went through everything that anybody ever could go through, and He came out victorious. He was "holy, harmless, undefiled, separate from sinners" (Heb. 7:26), and yet He was the friend of publicans and sinners.

In the Old Testament, the prophets were not mediators. The prophets did not stand between God and man and try to bring the two together. They announced what God had given them to announce. They were God's spokesmen. The priests were not really mediators because they themselves had to have a sacrifice for their own sins. They certainly could not bring God and man together permanently because nothing the Old Testament priests did had permanence to it. It was not until the Lord Jesus Christ came that the matter was settled completely. The Old Testament prophets could preach the Word, and the priests could carry on the ceremonies, but they could not permanently settle the problem of the enmity between God and man.

## Qualified in His Death

Jesus Christ is not only qualified to be a mediator in His Person, but He is qualified to be a mediator in His death. His death makes possible the removal of the enmity between God and man. "Who gave himself a ransom for all, to be testified in due time" (I Tim. 2:6).

This matter is dealt with in Hebrews 9:13-16: "For if the blood of bulls and of goats, and the ashes of an heifer sprinkling the unclean, sanctifieth to the purifying of the flesh: how much more shall the blood of Christ, who through the eternal Spirit offered himself without spot to God, purge your conscience from dead works to serve the living God? And for this cause he is the mediator of the new testament, that by means of death, for the redemption of the transgressions that were under the first testament, they which are called might receive the promise of eternal inheritance. For where a testament is, there must also of necessity be the death of the testator."

Under the Old Covenant there were various

ceremonies. The priests would shed the blood of animals and sprinkle it according to God's directions. They had special "holy water" made of the ashes of a heifer that had been offered. These various ceremonies gave outward sanctification—that is, they dealt with sin in a ceremonial way, but they could not change the heart.

The argument here is from the lesser to the greater. If the blood of bulls and goats and if the holy water which was sprinkled in the Old Testament era purified the flesh (outward sanctification), how much more shall the blood of Jesus Christ cleanse us? The blood of Jesus Christ works in the conscience and in the heart and takes away sin. "For this cause [because Jesus Christ has finished a perfect work on the cross] he is the mediator of the new testament [covenant]" (v. 15). In His work the Lord Jesus Christ is the perfect Mediator. As it were, when He was nailed to the cross, with one arm He reached up to heaven and touched God, and with the other arm He reached down to a needy world and touched sinners and brought the two together.

### Qualified in His Present Ministry

His present ministry in heaven today qualifies Him to be a Mediator. Hebrews 8:6 says, "But now hath he obtained a more excellent ministry, by how much also he is the mediator of a better covenant, which was established upon better promises."

The Old Testament high priest was not a mediator in the same sense as our Lord Jesus Christ. The

Old Covenant was a covenant of legal works; the New Covenant is one of faith and grace. The Old Covenant was external with washings and sacrifices which could only deal with external uncleanness. The New Covenant is internal: It deals with the inside of the person—the heart, the conscience. Under the Old Covenant, nothing was finished, but the New Covenant is completed. Jesus said, "It is finished" (John 19:30), and He is the guarantee that this covenant is going to stand.

In the New Testament world, a mediator not only brought people together, but a mediator also guaranteed the terms of the agreement. He would see to it that the terms of the agreement were met. In Hebrews 7:22 the Lord Jesus Christ is called the surety of a better testament. As long as He is alive in heaven, you and I have eternal salvation. Hebrews 7:25 says, "Wherefore he is able also to save them to the uttermost." It doesn't say "from the uttermost." It is true that He can save any lost sinner. But we are saved "to the uttermost," which means *eternally*. "Wherefore he is able also to save them to the uttermost that come unto God by him, seeing he ever liveth to make intercession for them" (v. 25). He is the Mediator in His present ministry, and He is all that we need.

### Definition of Mediation

Mediation is the ministry of Jesus Christ in bringing God and man together and settling the enmity once and for all, guaranteeing the terms of the agreement so that we are saved eternally.

## Not a Truce

Let's consider what mediation is not. It is not declaring a truce. A truce can always end. In Genesis 31 is the story of Laban and Jacob, two of the biggest schemers found anywhere in Scripture. It is difficult to know which was the better schemer. Jacob had run away and taken his family with him. Laban chased him, caught up with him and started an argument. They needed some kind of agreement. So they put up a heap of stones, and this heap of stones was called "Mizpah" (vv. 48,49), meaning "watchtower." "The Lord watch between me and thee, when we are absent one from another" (v. 49). This statement is often used as a benediction, but it really should not be. Let me explain why.

Do you know what Laban and Jacob were saying to each other? They were saying, "I don't trust you, and you don't trust me, so we're going to put up this heap of stones. Laban, don't you cross over the border; Jacob, don't you cross over the border. We can't watch each other, but the Lord is going to watch, and you had better keep the terms of the agreement." What a statement to use to close a church service! "We don't trust each other, but the Lord is going to watch between us." This is just declaring a truce. These men had been at odds with each other for more than 20 years; now they said, "Let's declare a truce and get it over with."

But that is not what mediation is. Mediation doesn't just declare a truce; *mediation ends the war*. Mediation removes the enmity. Jesus Christ bore the wrath of God for sin. Oh, the way they mistreated Him! And yet He lovingly, willingly died for us! Now He is the Mediator between God and man.

## Not Arguing With God

Mediation is not declaring a truce, nor is mediation an opportunity to argue with God. In Job 9:32,33, Job cried out for a daysman; that is, an umpire, a mediator, somebody who would represent him so that he could argue with God. He said, "How can I prove that I am right? I can't lay hands on God; He is too far away from me. I need somebody who can lay hands upon both of us." Who in the world could ever lay hands upon God? Only God could do that. Job was here crying out for the Lord Jesus Christ, the Mediator.

So mediation is not declaring a truce, and mediation is not an opportunity to argue with God. Mediation is the ministry of Jesus Christ in bringing us together with God and keeping us together and ministering to us from heaven.

## Peace With God

What does it mean in a practical way to have a Mediator in heaven? First of all, it means *peace with God.* "Therefore being justified by faith, we have peace with God" (Rom. 5:1). We are no longer at enmity with God. Jesus Christ has brought us together, and He is keeping us together. When you have peace with God, you have peace in your heart, no matter what trials may come.

## Acceptance With God

Second, it means *acceptance with God.* We know that we are accepted as long as Jesus Christ is alive in heaven as our Mediator. There is only one God and one Mediator. If there were two mediators, there wouldn't be peace. The church does not mediate between your soul and God. No religious person mediates between you and God; only Jesus Christ is the Mediator.

## Access to God and Security

Third, we have *access to God.* Because we have a Mediator in heaven, we are able to pray and intercede for others. Our intercession is based on His mediation.

Finally, it means *security.* We are secure because Jesus Christ, the Mediator, has finished the work. There is a beautiful picture of heaven in Hebrews 12:22: "Ye are come unto mount Sion, and unto the city of the living God, the heavenly Jerusalem." Verse 24 says, "To Jesus the mediator of the new covenant." He is in heaven administering the terms of the New Covenant. As long as He is there, we are saved and we are secure.

It is good to know we have a Mediator in heaven. Mediation is something you and I cannot do. Intercession is something we can share in, but not mediation. We can't come between God and man and settle the problem. We can pray and we can witness, but Jesus Christ is the only Mediator. Jesus said, "I am the way, the truth, and the life: no man cometh unto the Father, but by me" (John 14:6).

## Chapter 13

# Formed: The Believer's History

On the capitol dome in Washington, D.C., you will find the following inscription: "One God, one law, one element and one supreme event toward which the whole creation moves." What is that event? The inscription doesn't tell us. Is it the destruction of the world? Is it the establishing of a Communist state? Is it the bringing in of a perfect society? No. That one event toward which the whole creation is moving is the coming of our Lord Jesus Christ, at which time God's people will be conformed to Jesus Christ. Romans 8:29 says, "For whom he did foreknow, he also did predestinate to be conformed to the image of his Son."

You can summarize the history of the believer in the word "form." We are only clay. Clay cannot form itself; only God can form us. There are four stages in the life of every child of God. First, we were *formed* in God's image by God. Second, we were *deformed* from God's image by sin. Third, we are being *transformed* into God's image by the Spirit. Fourth, we shall one day be *conformed* to the Lord Jesus Christ when we see Him.

## Formed in God's Image

Let's examine this first stage in our spiritual experience: We were formed in God's image by God. "And the Lord God formed man of the dust of the ground, and breathed into his nostrils the breath of life; and man became a living soul" (Gen. 2:7). "So God created man in his own image, in the image of God created he him; male and female created he them" (1:27). What does it mean to be formed in God's image? It does not mean physical likeness because God is a spirit and does not have a body like we do. Some false religions try to teach us that God is physical and that man can one day become like God in that respect. The image of God means that we, like God, are a trinity—spirit, soul and body. God is a Trinity—Father, Son and Holy Spirit.

### Personality

But it means even more than that. It means *personality*. God is a person. God has a mind to think with, a heart to feel with and a will for decisions and action. Our personality is a reflection of the personality of God. Man basically is spiritual. In his material body, man is related to the earth; he came from dust. But in his spiritual makeup, he is related to God. He is both dust and deity, so to speak. We have both heaven and earth in our makeup, and God made us this way. We were formed in God's image by God.

This is an important doctrine in the Bible, and it has some very practical applications. If we were formed in God's image by God, then we have dignity—we are not just animals. Some people live like animals, and this is too bad, but we are not animals. Man was made in the image of God. He began with dignity, created by God in His image. This means that human life is valuable.

It is inconsistent for people who do not believe we were created by God in God's image to still want to exalt man. If man is just an animal, then why not let him live like an animal? Why have standards? Why have laws? Why does society have to have protection if we are only animals? It is inconsistent. The fact that we are made in God's image means we have dignity. We are not just animals.

### Responsibility

But it also means we have *responsibility*. We are responsible to God. He is the Creator, we are the creatures. The way you treat other people is a reflection of what you think about God because man was made in the image of God. We have no right to abuse or exploit other people because they, too, were made in the image of God.

### Destiny

It also means we have a special destiny. We were created by God in His image for a definite purpose. We are not here by accident, we are here by appointment. We are here to glorify God and to enjoy Him forever, as the catechism tells us. This explains why many people have such empty lives today. They don't realize this dignity, they don't fulfill this responsibility, and they are not prepared for this marvelous destiny.

### Deformed From God's Image

If we were formed in God's image by God, why then is everything in such a mess? Well, because we were deformed from God's image by sin. How else can you explain the chaos that the world is in today? Something in us cries out for God, and something else in us cries out for sin. Why is that? Because man fell, man is a sinner. When man fell into sin, his spirit died—he was separated from God. His soul was damaged; the image of God in him was damaged by sin. We no longer possess the kind of faculties that God gave us in the beginning. Something tragic has happened.

Ephesians 4:18,19 says, "Having the understanding darkened, being alienated from the life of God through the ignorance that is in them, because of the blindness of their heart: who being past feeling have given themselves over unto lasciviousness, to work all uncleanness with greediness." This is the result of sin. We were deformed from God's image by sin. The spirit died, and the soul has been damaged. The mind no longer thinks God's thoughts, the heart no longer loves God, the will no longer is submitted to God.

Of course, one day the body will die. God said to Adam and Eve, "In the day that thou eatest thereof thou shalt surely die" (Gen. 2:17). This is where death has come from. We came from the dust, we are going back to the dust, and we cannot help ourselves. Only God can make the difference.

## Transformed into God's Image

We were formed in God's image by God, and we were deformed from God's image by sin. But when we trust Jesus Christ as our Saviour, a miracle takes place. Our spirits become alive again, and God begins to work on our inner beings to make us more like Himself. We are being *transformed* into God's image by the Spirit.

Romans 12:1,2 says, "I beseech you therefore, brethren, by the mercies of God, that ye present your bodies a living sacrifice, holy, acceptable unto God, which is your reasonable service. And be not conformed to this world: but be ye transformed by the renewing of your mind, that ye may prove what is that good, and acceptable, and perfect, will of God." When you trust Christ as your Saviour, the Holy Spirit comes in, and you become a new creation. God starts all over again. "Therefore if any man be in Christ, he is a new creature: old things are passed away; behold, all things are become new" (II Cor. 5:17).

In Colossians 3:10 Paul wrote this: "[You] have put on the new man, which is renewed in knowledge after the image of him that created him." When you surrender to Jesus Christ as your Lord—give Him your body, your mind, your will and your heart—God begins to transform you.

Romans 12:2 says, "Be not conformed to this world: but be ye transformed by the renewing of your mind." The word "transformed" is the word "transfigure." In Matthew 17 our Lord was transfigured before His disciples. Transfiguration is a change on the outside that comes from the inside. You can change the outside with a masquerade costume, but masquerading has no place in the Christian life. Transformation is a change on the outside that comes from the inside. It is the work of the Holy Spirit.

This is why we read the Bible. As we read the Word of God, the Spirit of God transforms us and renews our mind. This is why we pray. I can't explain prayer. I have read many books on prayer, and I have studied it, but prayer to me is a continuous miracle. As we pray and fellowship with God, a transformation takes place in our character. Moses went up on the mountaintop and met with God. When he came down, his face was shining, but that glory eventually faded. You and I don't "borrow" glory and then lose it. We have the glory down inside. We are being transformed into God's image by the Holy Spirit.

This means we are *not* conforming to the world. Christians should not love the world or try to please the world. In our body, our mind, our will, our heart, we are trying, with the help of the Holy Spirit, to be more like the Lord Jesus Christ.

### Conformed to God's Image

We were formed in God's image by God, and we were deformed from God's image by sin. We are being transformed into God's image by the Spirit. One day we shall be *conformed* to God's image when we see Jesus Christ.

110

This is not some vague hope; this is an assurance based on God's Word. Romans 8:29 says, "For whom he did foreknow, he also did predestinate to be conformed to the image of his Son." "Our conversation [citizenship] is in heaven; from whence also we look for the Saviour, the Lord Jesus Christ: who shall change our vile body, that it may be fashioned like unto his glorious body" (Phil. 3:20,21). One day we shall be like the Lord Jesus Christ, for we shall see Him as He is.

That is the blessed hope of the believer. In fact, we have already been glorified. Notice Romans 8:30: "Moreover whom he did predestinate, them he also called: and whom he called, them he also justified: and whom he justified, them he also glorified." Glorified—already completed! Jesus said, "The glory which thou gavest me I have given them" (John 17:22). When we see the Lord Jesus Christ, we shall be conformed to His image.

Let's not be conformed to the world. That is such a waste of time and energy, and you miss so many blessings. All history is moving in the direction of the coming of Jesus Christ. Let God transform you daily. Let the Holy Spirit use the Word of God to transform your mind. Yield to Him, and look forward to the coming of the Lord Jesus. Whatever your weaknesses and problems may be, just remember that one day you and I shall be conformed to God's image when we see Jesus Christ. But let's not wait until then. Let's start being transformed by the Lord Jesus Christ today by letting the Spirit of God have His way.

## Chapter 14

# Predestination: God's Plan for His Own

God has made this universe to operate a day at a time. And you and I are supposed to live a day at a time. God's promise is "As thy days, so shall thy strength be" (Deut. 33:25). You and I are able to live a day at a time because of the fact that God is in control.

Have you ever walked into a group of people in the middle of a conversation and felt uneasy because you did not know what was going on? Have you ever started to read in the middle of a book? When we walk into the middle of something such as that, we get frustrated because we are not sure what's going on.

Many people today are not sure what is going on. Change is taking place so rapidly and so radically these days that people are afraid. Some people are even rebellious. Rebellion, after all, is fear turned inside out. Some people become sick or nervous from life's pressures and then withdraw, using their illness as an excuse. Some people even commit suicide because they cannot take the pressures of life.

For life to be meaningful, we have to know where we came from, why we are here and where we are going. Of course, many people have philosophies that try to give those facts. The Communist talks about economic forces and class struggle. The evolutionist has his solution to the problem in his doctrine of the survival of the fittest. The agnostic says, "Well, we just don't know; we're living by chance or by luck. Enjoy today because tomorrow may not come. Do your own thing." He has a fatalistic philosophy of life. And then we have the people who are superstitious. They study the stars, they consult astrological charts, they might even dabble in the occult. But the Christian doesn't need any of this because the Christian has his Bible, and the Bible teaches us that God is in control.

What I want to share with you is all wrapped up in the word "predestination." The minute you mention that word, some people get nervous because right in the middle of predestination is the word "destiny." It sounds so fatalistic, it sounds so frightening. The Christian is not afraid of life. He is not afraid to live a day at a time because he has his confidence in God and knows that God is in control.

Romans 8:28-30 says, "And we know that all things work together for good to them that love God, to them who are the called according to his purpose. For whom he did foreknow, he also did predestinate to be conformed to the image of his Son, that he might be the firstborn among many brethren. Moreover whom he did predestinate,

113

them he also called: and whom he called, them he also justified: and whom he justified, them he also glorified."

We have in these three verses God's wonderful plan for His people. We are going to study this word "predestinate" because when you understand it, you will be able to relax and not worry about what is going on around you.

The word "predestinate" is used only six times in the New Testament. It is not always translated that way. It is the Greek word *proorizo*. You say, "Well, what does that mean?" *Pro* means "beforehand," and *orizo* means "to mark out." Our word "horizon" comes from that word. The horizon is that area marked out before us that separates the sky from the land.

Let's answer three questions about predestination, and in answering these questions, calm our fears and assure our hearts.

### What Does Predestination Mean?

Question number one: *What does predestination mean?* Predestination is God's eternal plan to make His own children like the Lord Jesus Christ. The English prefix "pre" means beforehand, and "destinate" means destiny. "Predestination" means a destination planned beforehand. Predestination simply affirms that God has an eternal plan for His children. The destiny He has planned for them is that they shall be like the Lord Jesus Christ. "For whom he did foreknow, he also did predestinate to be conformed to the image of his Son" (Rom. 8:29).

114

You should note some important facts about predestination. First of all, predestination applies only to the saved. I do not know any place in the Bible where it says that God predestines people to go to hell. I do not find any place in the Word of God where we are told that God predestines people to be lost. Quite the contrary is true. He tells us to go into *all* the world and preach the Gospel.

Does the Bible teach election? It certainly does. "He hath chosen us in him [Christ] before the foundation of the world" (Eph. 1:4). Does this mean that we cannot share the Gospel with everybody? No, it doesn't. You and I do not know who God's elect are. Predestination teaches us that God's elect one day are going to be like the Lord Jesus Christ. There is not a single verse that I know of in Scripture which says that God has predestined people to go to hell.

Two contrasting verses are found in Matthew 25. Verse 34 says, "Then shall the King say unto them on his right hand [saved people], Come, ye blessed of my Father, inherit the kingdom prepared for you from the foundation of the world." In verse 41 we read: "Then shall he say also unto them on the left hand [lost people], Depart from me, ye cursed, into everlasting fire, prepared for the devil and his angels." Verse 41 does not say, "Prepared for you from before the foundation of the world." He did say to the saved that the kingdom had been prepared for them from the foundation of the world.

Predestination comes from the heart of a loving Father. We must never think of predestination as some cold program that God worked out in the distant glories of eternity. Ephesians 1:4,5 says, "According as he hath chosen us in him before the foundation of the world, that we should be holy and without blame before him in love: having predestinated us unto the adoption of children by Jesus Christ." How has He predestinated us? *In love.* Predestination is the wise plan of a loving Father, and He is going to work out His plan.

Something else is true. Predestination is only *part* of the total plan. Five key factors are mentioned in Romans 8:29,30, and we should look at them in some detail.

### How Does Predestination Work?

Question number two: *How does predestination work?* According to Romans 8:29 predestination begins with foreknowledge: "Whom he did foreknow, he also did predestinate." Foreknowledge does not simply mean "to know beforehand." There are those who teach that God knew beforehand who would believe; therefore, He predestinated them to be saved. That's backward. If God only *foresees* future events, then what makes these events certain? An event must be made certain before it can be known as certain, and only God can make events certain.

To foreknow means *to choose beforehand, to set your love upon someone.* This is all by God's grace. God in His grace sets His love upon, He sets His heart upon, certain ones who are going to be saved.

116

That is where it all begins—with God's gracious foreknowledge.

Either salvation is by grace, totally from the loving heart of God, or there is no salvation at all.

God sets His love upon, He sets His heart upon, certain ones. These certain ones are predestinated, then, to be conformed to the image of Christ. Of course, this involved the death of Christ, and even that was predestined. Acts 4:27,28 says, "For of a truth against thy holy child Jesus, whom thou hast anointed, both Herod, and Pontius Pilate, with the Gentiles, and the people of Israel, were gathered together, for to do whatsoever thy hand and thy counsel determined before to be done." The death of Christ was not an accident; it was predestined by a loving Father.

Predestination simply means that one day you are going to be like Jesus Christ. It begins with foreknowledge, and it involves being *called* by the Holy Spirit. Romans 8:30 says, "Moreover whom he did predestinate, them he also called." This calling comes through human agency.

Don't ever get the idea that because God has elected some and these whom He has elected are predestined to go to heaven, that Christians should do nothing. "But we are bound to give thanks alway to God for you, brethren beloved of the Lord, because God hath from the beginning chosen you to salvation through sanctification of the Spirit and belief of the truth: whereunto he called you by our gospel, to the obtaining of the glory of our Lord Jesus Christ" (II Thess. 2:13,14). Those whom God

117

elects and foreknows, He predestines, and those whom He predestines, He calls. That is why we have a ministry of sharing the Word of God. That is why we witness and pray.

Those who are called and who respond to that call are justified—declared righteous. Those whom He justifies, He also glorifies. Again notice the past tense of that verb: "And whom he justified, them he also glorified" (Rom. 8:30).

This is God's total plan. What begins with foreknowledge ends with glory. Predestination simply declares that God's people are going to make it—they will one day be conformed to the image of Christ.

### What Does Predestination Mean Today?

Now our third question: *What does predestination mean to us today as believers?* Please keep in mind that Paul wrote Romans to ordinary people, common people, not theologians, not philosophers. The theologians wrestle with some of these things, but Paul did not write Romans to theologians. He wrote for common people, and he knew they could understand it if they would just open their heart to the Spirit.

#### Salvation Is Bigger Than We Think

What does predestination mean to us today? First of all, it means that *salvation is much bigger than what we think.* Your salvation is not a minor incident; it is part of an eternal plan. God is so gracious that, from all eternity, He has planned that we shall be conformed to the image of His Son. Don't ever allow salvation to become a minor thing. It is a big thing, far bigger than we realize. It is a part of a great eternal plan.

## God Is Bigger Than Our Trials

Second, predestination means that *God is much bigger than our trials and our troubles*. Notice Romans 8:31: "What shall we then say to these things?" What things? The facts that we are foreknown, predestined, called, justified and already glorified. "If God be for us, who can be against us?" In the rest of Romans 8 Paul spelled out so beautifully that God is bigger than all of our sufferings and trials.

You may hurt today. Things may be falling apart today. But I want you to know that if you are saved, you are a part of something eternal and big and wonderful and glorious. God is bigger than any trouble you may go through.

## No Christian Will Be Lost

Third, it means that *no true Christian will ever be lost*. There can be no separation from God. God started this great salvation, and God is going to see it to completion. God knew what was happening long before these things ever took place. I cannot believe that any true Christian can ever be lost because he is a part of a great eternal plan.

God's plan of salvation was secure from all eternity. The Lamb was slain from before the foundation of the world (see Rev. 13:8). God is not caught by surprise. God is not depending on your strength or mine. "Whom he justified, them he also glorified" (Rom. 8:30). God is so sure that we are going to heaven, He has already glorified us. All we are waiting for is the revelation of that glory.

## We Live by Faith

This leads us to a fourth application: *We have to live by faith, not by sight.* God knows what He is doing. Jacob was walking by sight when he said, "All these things are against me" (Gen. 42:36). Really, everything was working *for* him. So walk by faith, not by sight, and let God have His way.

## We Must Obey God

Finally, *we must obey God and share in His purpose.* He is working out His beautiful plan in your life, so don't be afraid, and don't be alarmed. God has everything all taken care of. Just trust Him, obey Him and walk with Him. Pray and believe, and one of these days, with all of God's people, you will end up in heaven—glorified!

## Chapter 15

# Glorification: Completion of God's Plan

One balmy summer day my wife and I visited one of the most famous cemeteries in the world. This cemetery is located at Stoke Poges, not far from Windsor Castle in England. It was there that Thomas Gray wrote his famous poem "Elegy Written in a Country Churchyard." Perhaps you had to read that poem and memorize part of it when you were in school. As I stood there among those ancient graves, one stanza of that poem came to my mind:

> The boast of heraldry, the pomp of pow'r,
> And all that beauty, all that wealth e'er gave,
> Awaits alike the inevitable hour:
> The paths of glory lead but to the grave.

Thomas Gray was right when he wrote that. As far as man is concerned, all of his glory ends at the grave. "Being born again, not of corruptible seed, but of incorruptible, by the word of God, which liveth and abideth for ever. For all flesh is as grass, and all the glory of man as the flower of grass. The grass withereth, and the flower thereof falleth away: but the word of the Lord endureth for ever. And this is the word which by the gospel is preached unto

121

you" (I Pet. 1:23-25). Man's glory does not last because man's glory has been stained by sin.

Man once walked with God and shared in God's glory, but now "all have sinned, and come short of the glory of God" (Rom. 3:23). Glorification is an important doctrine in the Bible. The glory of God simply means the sum total of all that God is, the expression of His essence. Glory is the result of all that God does. Only God has glory, and only God deserves glory. But as Christians, we share in the glory of God. Romans 5:2 says, "By whom also we have access by faith into this grace wherein we stand, and rejoice in hope of the glory of God." Romans 8:30 says, "Whom he justified, them he also glorified." You and I, as believers, share in the glory of God.

## God Completes His Eternal Plan

What does this doctrine of glorification really mean? It means, first of all, *that God completes His eternal plan.* I trust as we have been studying the key words of the Christian life you have discovered that salvation is not some minor incident in history. Salvation is part of a great plan established from eternity. Your salvation is not an accident; your salvation is not some little thing. Your salvation is part of God's great eternal plan, and the end of that plan is glorification. "Whom he justified, them he also glorified" (Rom. 8:30).

In Ephesians 1, Paul reminded us three times that salvation is for God's glory. In verse 6 he said, "To the praise of the glory of his grace, wherein he hath made us accepted in the beloved." Verse 12 says, "That we should be to the praise of his glory." Verse 14 says, "Which is the earnest of our inheritance until the redemption of the purchased possession, unto the praise of his glory."

One of these days the Lord Jesus Christ is going to return and put everything together. The Devil is busy tearing everything apart, and he has a great deal of help from sinners. But one day the Lord Jesus Christ is going to put everything together. Ephesians 1:9,10 tells us, "Having made known unto us the mystery of his will, according to his good pleasure which he hath purposed in himself: that in the dispensation of the fulness of times he might gather together in one all things in Christ, both which are in heaven, and which are on earth; even in him." Jesus Christ is going to gather everything together, and we are going to enter into glory.

The greatest purpose possible in all of the universe is the glory of God, not the glory of man. Man does not have anything worth glorying about. When God does things for His own glory, He is not being selfish or egotistical. There is none higher than God, there is none greater than God. If anyone who is less than God were glorified, it would not be right. God, being as great as He is, deserves all glory and all praise and all honor.

In fact, this is what they are singing about in heaven. "Thou art worthy, O Lord, to receive glory and honour and power: for thou hast created all things, and for thy pleasure they are and were created" (Rev. 4:11). Can you look at any human

123

being and say, "You are worthy to receive glory and honor"? "Saying with a loud voice, Worthy is the Lamb that was slain to receive power, and riches, and wisdom, and strength, and honour, and glory, and blessing" (5:12). You can find no higher purpose in the universe than the glory of God. Glorification means that God completes His eternal plan.

If you are going through suffering now, I want to remind you that, according to the Bible, suffering leads to glory. "But the God of all grace, who hath called us unto his eternal glory by Christ Jesus, after that ye have suffered a while" (I Pet. 5:10). "For I reckon that the sufferings of this present time are not worthy to be compared with the glory which shall be revealed in us" (Rom. 8:18). We suffer here, but it means glory over there, and God is going to compensate for all our suffering.

Keep in mind that the greatest purpose in all the world is the glory of God. Glorification means that God completes His eternal plan. Jesus didn't die just to rescue people from sin. Nor did He die on the cross just to change people's lives and put their homes back together again. *He died so that God might be glorified.* When you are busy in the work of evangelism, keep in mind that it is not for the purpose of counting results. It is not for the purpose of advertising statistics. It is for the purpose of glorifying God.

### Christ Is Rewarded for His Sacrifice

Glorification means that God completes His eternal plan. It also means that *Christ is rewarded for His sacrificial work.* In Jude 1:24 we read: "Now unto him that is able to keep you from falling, and to present you faultless before the presence of his glory with exceeding joy." The Lord Jesus Christ, one of these days, is going to present His Church before the Father with exceeding joy. This ties in with Hebrews 12:2: "Who for the joy that was set before him endured the cross." What was the joy that was set before Him? The joy of one day bringing His Bride to glory.

Our Lord Jesus did not only suffer physically on the cross. Other people were crucified and suffered pain. But He also suffered *spiritually.* He was made sin for you and me. Our Lord Jesus Christ went through the agonies of hell for us. What is His reward for this? His reward is glory in the Church throughout all eternity.

When our Lord Jesus Christ returns, we are going to share with Him in glory. Second Thessalonians 1:10 says, "When he shall come to be glorified in his saints, and to be admired in all them that believe." He is going to be glorified in His saints. Glorification means that God completes His eternal plan and that Christ is rewarded for His sacrificial work.

### Christians' Salvation Shall Be Fulfilled

Glorification also means that *Christians shall experience the fulfillment of their salvation.* Being born again is just the beginning. When you trust Christ as your Saviour, that is just the beginning—the best is yet to come!

125

In Romans 8:30 we discover that the ultimate experience is glorification: "Whom he justified, them he also glorified." Romans 8:19-23 points out the fact that, in this life, we go through trial and suffering. "For the earnest expectation of the creature waiteth for the manifestation of the sons of God" (v. 19). There are a lot of big words in that verse. What he is saying is that all of creation is standing eagerly on tiptoe, waiting for us to be glorified. Why? *When we are glorified, then creation will be set free from the bondage of sin.* Christians will experience the fulfillment of their salvation.

To begin with, this means a new body. God is not saving bodies today. He is rescuing our bodies from sin, and He is using our bodies for His glory, but the major ministry God has today is not for the body. The redemption of our bodies is still in the future. God is majoring on building character, building the spiritual life to glorify God. But one day we are going to get new bodies. This corruption is going to put on incorruption, and this body of humiliation is going to put on glory. One day we shall receive a glorified body like Christ's body. God saves the total person. God doesn't just save souls, God doesn't just save spirits. God saves the total person. One day we shall be totally redeemed.

It also means a new environment, a brand-new home. When you get discouraged, sit down and read Revelation 21 and 22. John said, "I saw a new heaven and a new earth: for the first heaven and the first earth were passed away; and there was no more sea. And I John saw the holy city, new Jerusalem, coming down from God out of heaven, prepared as a bride adorned for her husband. And I heard a great voice out of heaven saying, Behold, the tabernacle of God is with men, and he will dwell with them, and they shall be his people, and God himself shall wipe away all tears from their eyes; and there shall be no more death, neither sorrow, nor crying, neither shall there be any more pain: for the former things are passed away" (21:1-4). Glorification means that we are going to enter a brand-new environment.

When God glorifies our bodies, He has to give us a glorious home to live in, and that glorious home is heaven. Heaven is a place of no pain, no death, no darkness, no sorrow, no crying. It is a place where you will never find a mortuary or a cemetery, a place where there will be no hospitals or pharmacies, a place where no tear will ever fall and no doubt will ever cloud the skies. It will be a place of glorious reunion when we meet with the Lord Jesus Christ and our loved ones who have gone before. Glorification means a new home, a new environment.

### A New Ministry

And finally, glorification means *a new ministry.* If you have the idea that heaven is simply a place of clouds and harps and robes, you had better wake up because Revelation 7:15 tells me, "Therefore are they before the throne of God, and serve him day and night in his temple."

I don't know what we are going to do throughout all eternity, but it is going to be wonderful. A whole

127

universe will be opened to us. Different people have speculated about our ministry in heaven, but I am not going to speculate. All I know is that we are going to serve Him. That's why He saved us. We are going to have all eternity to grow in our knowledge of God, coming to understand His truth in a deeper way. We are going to experience the fellowship of the angels and the patriarchs and the saints of God, and we are going to enter into a new ministry. He is preparing us for our ministry now. You may wonder, "Why am I going through this time of trial?" He is preparing you for glory.

The doctrine of glorification gives me a great feeling of security. God is going to finish what He started, and God is going to glorify His Church. It gives me great encouragement in times of suffering. As we go through times of difficulty, we can look up because we know Jesus is coming. We know that our suffering today is not worthy to be compared with the glory that shall be revealed in us (see Rom. 8:18). To me glorification means security, encouragement in suffering and a motivation for service.

"Therefore, my beloved brethren, be ye stedfast, unmoveable, always abounding in the work of the Lord" (I Cor. 15:58). That admonition is at the end of a great chapter on resurrection and future glory. Keep on serving. Don't give up—the best is yet to come. God's plan will be completed, and you and I are going to share in the total blessing of glory in heaven someday.